REA's *interactive flashcards*™

ENGLISH VOCABULARY
Set #2 (More Great Words)

**Staff of Research and Education Association,
Dr. M. Fogiel, Director**

 Research & Education Association
61 Ethel Road West
Piscataway, New Jersey 08854

REA's INTERACTIVE FLASHCARDS™
ENGLISH VOCABULARY
Set #2 (More Great Words)

Printed in the United States of America

Library of Congress Catalog Card Number 98-66638

International Standard Book Number 0-87891-235-5

Research & Education Association, Piscataway, New Jersey 08854

REA's Interactive Flashcards

What they're for

How to use them

They come in a book, not in a box of hundreds of loose cards.

They are most useful as test time approaches to help you check your test readiness.

They are a good tool for self-study and also for group study. They can even be used as a competitive game to see who scores best.

They work with any text.

The interactive feature is a unique learning tool. With it, you can write in your own answer to each question which you can then check against the correct answer provided on the flip side of each card.

You will find that the flashcards in a book have several advantages over flashcards in a box.

You don't have to cope with hundreds of loose cards. Whenever you want to study, you don't have to decide beforehand which cards you are likely to need; you don't have to pull them out of a box (and later return them in their proper place). You can just open the book and get going without ado.

A very detailed index will guide you to whatever topics you want to cover.

A number of blank card pages is included, in case you want to construct some of your own Q's and A's.

You can take along REA's flashcard book anywhere, ready for use when you are. You don't need to tote along the box or a bunch of loose cards.

REA's Flashcard books have been carefully put together with REA's customary concern for quality. We believe you will find them an excellent review and study tool.

Dr. M. Fogiel
Program Director

P.S. As you could tell, you could see all the flashcards in the book while you were in the store; they aren't sealed in shrink-wrap.

HOW TO USE THE FLASHCARDS IN THIS BOOK

This book contains over 700 vocabulary words with their definitions, parts of speech, and sample sentences. The vocabulary words were chosen from all levels of difficulty. This allows students to use this book to study for any vocabulary test, in any grade.

Each question presents a vocabulary word. The answer to the question includes the part of speech of the word being defined, the definition of the word, and a sample sentence using the vocabulary word in context.

Here is an example:

Question:

PERILOUS

Answer:

adj. dangerous; involving peril or risk

The hikers took caution while crossing the perilous peaks.

Questions

Q1

FECUND

*Your Own Answer*_____

Q2

MERCURIAL

*Your Own Answer*_____

Q3

COAGULATE

*Your Own Answer*_____

Correct Answers

A1

adj.—intellectually productive; prolific

The artist felt the **fecund** time of his career was the early 1980s, when he produced some of his best work.

A2

adj.—quick, changeable, fickle

The **mercurial** youth changed outfits six times before deciding what to wear.

A3

v.—to become a semisolid, soft mass; to clot

The liquid will **coagulate** and close the tube if left standing.

Questions

ACRID

*Your Own Answer*_____

BERATE

*Your Own Answer*_____

FACSIMILE

*Your Own Answer*_____

Correct Answers

A4

adj.—sharp; bitter; foul smelling

Although the soup is a healthy food choice, it is so **acrid** not many people choose to eat it.

A5

v.—to scold; to reprove; to reproach; to criticize

The child was **berated** by her parents for breaking the china.

A6

n.—copy; reproduction; replica

The **facsimile** of the elaborate painting was indistinguishable from the original.

Questions

Q7

DITHER

*Your Own Answer*_____

_____

Q8

INDUBITABLY

*Your Own Answer*_____

_____

Q9

ENDUE

*Your Own Answer*_____

_____

Correct Answers

A7

v.; n.—1. to act indecisively 2. a confused condition

1. She **dithered** every time she had to make a decision.

2. Having to take two tests in one day left the student in a **dither**.

A8

adj.—unquestionably; surely

The officer was **indubitably** the best candidate for captain.

A9

v.—to provide

The philanthropist agreed to **endue** the hospital with the necessary funding.

Questions

ERUDITE

*Your Own Answer*_____

Q11

MOROSE

*Your Own Answer*_____

Q12

WHEEDLE

*Your Own Answer*_____

Correct Answers

A10

adj.—having a wide knowledge acquired through reading

The woman was so **erudite**, she could recite points on most any subject.

A11

adj.—moody, despondent

He was **morose** over the death of his beloved pet.

A12

v.—to influence or persuade

The crook may attempt to **wheedle** the money from the bank.

Questions

SCRUTINIZE

*Your Own Answer*_____

MOLLIFY

*Your Own Answer*_____

DUPLICITY

*Your Own Answer*_____

Correct Answers

A13

v.—to examine closely; to study

After allowing his son to borrow the family car, the father **scrutinized** every section for dents.

A14

v.—to soften; to make less intense

We used our hands to **mollify** the sound of our giggling.

A15

n.—deception

She forgave his **duplicity** but divorced him anyway.

Questions

Q16

SKEPTIC

*Your Own Answer*_____

Q17

PARSE

*Your Own Answer*_____

Q18

MEANDER

*Your Own Answer*_____

Correct Answers

n.—doubter

Even after seeing evidence that his competitor's new engine worked, the engineer remained a **skeptic** that it was marketable.

v.—to separate (a sentence) into parts and describe the function of each

An English teacher may ask a student to **parse** a sentence.

v.; adj.—1. to wind, to wander 2. winding, wandering aimlessly

1. The stream **meanders** through the valley.

2. Because we took a long, **meandering** walk, we arrived home well after dark.

Questions

Q19

WAFT

*Your Own Answer*_____

Q20

MACULATE

*Your Own Answer*_____

Q21

IMMINENT

*Your Own Answer*_____

Correct Answers

A19

v.—to move gently by wind or breeze
The smoke **wafted** out of the chimney.

A20

adj.; v.—1. spotted, blotched 2. hence defiled,
impure (opposite: immaculate); to stain, spot,
defile
1. The **maculate** rug could not be cleaned.
2. Grape juice **maculated** the carpet.

A21

adj.—likely to happen without delay
The storm clouds warned of the **imminent**
downpour.

Questions

Q22

RESILIENT

*Your Own Answer*_____

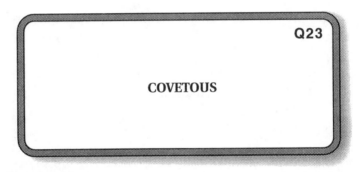

Q23

COVETOUS

*Your Own Answer*_____

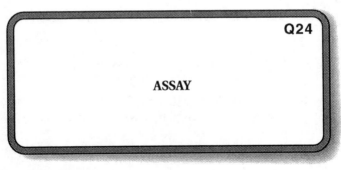

Q24

ASSAY

*Your Own Answer*_____

Correct Answers

A22

adj.—flexible; capable of withstanding stress

The elderly man attributed his **resilient** health to a good diet and frequent exercise.

A23

adj.—greedy; very desirous

Lonnie, **covetous** of his brother's girlfriend, decided to romantically pursue her.

A24

v.; n.—1. to test; to analyze 2. an examination or test; the results of an examination or test

1. Have the soil **assayed.**
2. The **assay** of the soil sample was inconclusive.

Questions

Q25

INCESSANT

*Your Own Answer*_____

Q26

FERVENT

*Your Own Answer*_____

Q27

TERMAGANT

*Your Own Answer*_____

Correct Answers

A25

adj.—constant and unending

The mother gave in to the child after her **incessant** crying.

A26

adj.—passionate; intense

They have a **fervent** relationship that keeps them together every minute of every day.

A27

n.—a constantly quarrelsome woman

The character Kate in Shakespeare's *The Taming of the Shrew* is a classic example of a **termagant**.

Questions

Q28

DISCOMFIT

*Your Own Answer*_____

Q29

INTANGIBLE

*Your Own Answer*_____

Q30

EQUINOX

*Your Own Answer*_____

Correct Answers

A28

v.—to frustrate the expectations of
The close game **discomfited** the number one
player.

A29

adj.—incapable of being touched; immaterial
Intangible though it may be, sometimes just
knowing that the work you do helps others is
reward enough.

A30

n.—precise time when day and night are of
equal length
On the **equinox** we had twelve hours of night
and day.

Questions

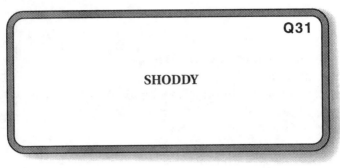

Q31

SHODDY

*Your Own Answer*_____

_____

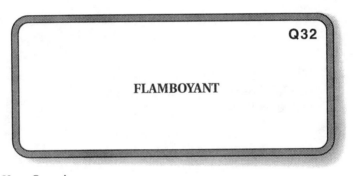

Q32

FLAMBOYANT

*Your Own Answer*_____

_____

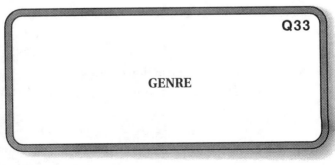

Q33

GENRE

*Your Own Answer*_____

_____

Correct Answers

A31

adj.—of inferior quality; cheap

The state's attorney said many homes, as they were built with **shoddy** materials, were bound to just blow apart even in winds of 60 or 70 miles per hour.

A32

adj.—being too showy or ornate

The **flamboyant** nature of the couple was evident in their loud clothing.

A33

adj.—designating a type of film or book

The **genre** of the book is historical fiction.

Questions

Q34

DESOLATE

*Your Own Answer*_____

Q35

FESTER

*Your Own Answer*_____

Q36

FLINCH

*Your Own Answer*_____

Correct Answers

A34

adj.—to be left alone or made lonely

Driving down the **desolate** road had Kelvin worried that he wouldn't reach a gas station in time.

A35

v.—to become more and more virulent and fixed

His anger **festered** until no one could change his mind.

A36

v.—to wince; to draw back; to retreat

The older brother made his younger sister **flinch** when he jokingly tried to punch her arm.

Questions

Q37

OBLOQUY

*Your Own Answer*_____

Q38

MISCREANT

*Your Own Answer*_____

Q39

RUFFIAN

*Your Own Answer*_____

Correct Answers

A37

n.—widespread condemnation or abuse; disgrace or infamy resulting from this

The child suffered quite an **obloquy** at the hands of his classmates.

A38

adj.; n.—1. evil 2. an evil person, villain

1. Her **miscreant** actions shocked and surprised her family.

2. The **miscreant** thought nothing of taking others' money and belongings.

A39

n.—a tough person or a hoodlum

Contrary to popular opinion, **ruffians** are nothing new in the city.

Questions

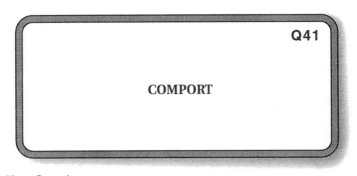

Q40

LUCENT

*Your Own Answer*_____

Q41

COMPORT

*Your Own Answer*_____

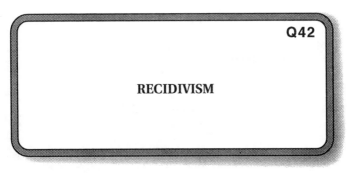

Q42

RECIDIVISM

*Your Own Answer*_____

Correct Answers

A40

adj.—shining; translucent

The flowing garment gave the woman a **lucent** quality when standing in the spotlight.

A41

v.—fitting in with; to behave

It was easy to **comport** to the new group of employees.

A42

n.—habitual or chronic relapse of criminal or antisocial offenses

Even after intense therapy the parolee experienced several episodes of **recidivism**, and was eventually sent back to prison.

Questions

Q43

UNALLOYED

*Your Own Answer*_____

Q44

TRADUCE

*Your Own Answer*_____

Q45

INTERCEDE

*Your Own Answer*_____

Correct Answers

A43

adj.—pure, of high quality

An **unalloyed** chain is of greater value than a piece of costume jewelry.

A44

v.—to defame or slander

His actions **traduced** his reputation.

A45

v.—to plead on behalf of another; to mediate

The superpowers were called on to **intercede** in the talks between the two warring nations.

Questions

Q46

HYBRID

*Your Own Answer*_____

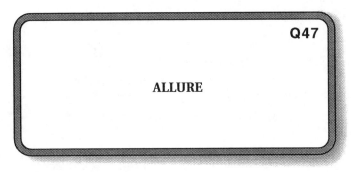

Q47

ALLURE

*Your Own Answer*_____

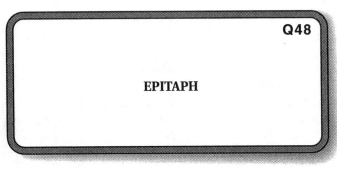

Q48

EPITAPH

*Your Own Answer*_____

Correct Answers

A46

n.—anything of mixed origin

The flower was a **hybrid** of three different flowers.

A47

v.; n.—1. to attract, entice 2. attraction, temptation or glamour

1. The romantic young man **allured** the beautiful woman by preparing a wonderful dinner.

2. Singapore's **allure** is its bustling economy.

A48

n.—an inscription on a monument in honor or memory of a dead person

The **epitaph** described the actions of a brave man.

Questions

Q49

DETER

*Your Own Answer*_____

Q50

INTREPID

*Your Own Answer*_____

Q51

SATIRE

*Your Own Answer*_____

Correct Answers

A49

v.—to prevent; to discourage, hinder

He **deterred** the rabbits by putting down garlic around the garden.

A50

adj.—fearless, bold

The **intrepid** photographer flew on some of the fiercest bombing raids of the war.

A51

n.—a novel or play that uses humor or irony to expose folly

The new play was a **satire** that exposed the president's inability to lead the country.

Questions

Q52

ERADICATION

*Your Own Answer*_____

Q53

LUMINOUS

*Your Own Answer*_____

Q54

VERSATILE

*Your Own Answer*_____

Correct Answers

n.—the act of annihilating, destroying, or erasing

Some have theorized that the **eradication** of dinosaurs was due to a radical change in climate.

adj.—emitting light; shining; also enlightened or intelligent

The **luminous** quality of the precious stone made it look like a fallen star.

adj.—having many uses; multifaceted

Clay is a **versatile** material, since it can be shaped into so many different objects.

Questions

Q55

LAGGARD

*Your Own Answer*_____

Q56

DEBACLE

*Your Own Answer*_____

Q57

STAID

*Your Own Answer*_____

Correct Answers

A55

n.; adj.—1. a person who has fallen behind
2. moving slowly

1. The **laggard** was lost in the crowd.
2. The train was **laggard**.

A56

n.—a disaster; a collapse; a rout

The Securities and Exchange Commission and
the stock exchanges implemented numerous
safeguards to head off another **debacle** on Wall
Street.

A57

adj.—marked by self-control
The horse was **staid** as it entered the stable.

Questions

Q58

FETTER

*Your Own Answer*_____

Q59

VOUCHSAFE

*Your Own Answer*_____

Q60

ECCENTRIC

*Your Own Answer*_____

Correct Answers

A58

n.; v.—1. a chain to bind the feet 2. to bind with shackles or chains

1. A **fetter** kept the dog chained to the fence.
2. The cowboy **fettered** the horse to keep her from escaping.

A59

v.—to be gracious enough to grant; to guarantee as safe

The owner of the property agreed to **vouchsafe** our use of her land.

A60

adj.—odd; peculiar; strange

People like to talk with the **eccentric** artist since he has such different views on everyday subjects.

Questions

DISPASSIONATE

*Your Own Answer*_____

COMELINESS

Q62

*Your Own Answer*_____

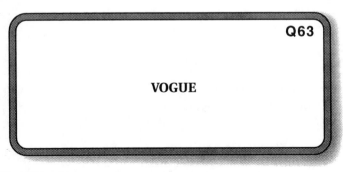

VOGUE

Q63

*Your Own Answer*_____

Correct Answers

adj.—lack of feeling; impartial

She was a very emotional person and could not work with such a **dispassionate** employer.

n.—beauty; attractiveness in appearance or behavior

The **comeliness** of the woman attracted everyone's attention.

n.—modern fashion

Women's magazines advertise the clothing they believe to be in **vogue**.

Questions

Q64

CONCILIATORY

*Your Own Answer*_____

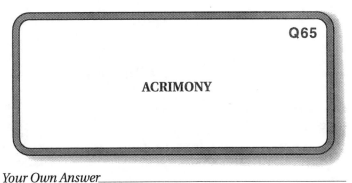

Q65

ACRIMONY

*Your Own Answer*_____

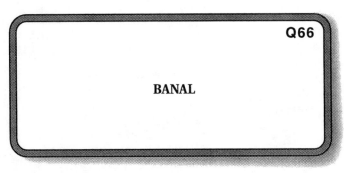

Q66

BANAL

*Your Own Answer*_____

Correct Answers

A64

adj.—tending to conciliate or reconcile

The diplomat sought to take a **conciliatory** approach to keep the talks going.

A65

n.—sharpness or bitterness in language or manner

The **acrimony** of her response was shocking.

A66

adj.—trite; without freshness or originality

Attending parties became **banal** after a few weeks.

Questions

Q67

CIRCUMSPECT

*Your Own Answer*_____

Q68

CURB

*Your Own Answer*_____

Q69

PROFOUND

*Your Own Answer*_____

Correct Answers

A67

adj.—considering all circumstances

A **circumspect** decision must be made when so many people are involved.

A68

n.; v.—1. a restraint or framework 2. to restrain; to control

1. A **curb** was put up along the street to help drainage.
2. The addict continued to attempt to **curb** his habit.

A69

adj.—deep; knowledgeable; thorough

It was with **profound** regret and sorrow that the family had to leave their homeland for a more prosperous country.

Questions

Q70

BUMPTIOUS

*Your Own Answer*_____

Q71

CAVIL

*Your Own Answer*_____

Q72

COMMISERATE

*Your Own Answer*_____

Correct Answers

A70

adj.—arrogant

He was **bumptious** in manner as he approached the podium to accept his anticipated award.

A71

v.—to bicker

The siblings are constantly **caviling**, which drives their parents crazy.

A72

v.—to show sympathy for

The hurricane victims **commiserated** each other about the loss of their homes.

Questions

FACETIOUS

*Your Own Answer*_____

DISTENTION

*Your Own Answer*_____

INGENUOUS

*Your Own Answer*_____

Correct Answers

A73

adj.—joking in an awkward or improper manner

His **facetious** sarcasm was inappropriate during his first staff meeting.

A74

n.—inflation or extension

The bulge in the carpet was caused by the **distention** of the wood underneath.

A75

adj.—noble; honorable; candid; also naive, simple, artless, without guile

The **ingenuous** doctor had a great bedside manner, especially when it came to laying out the full implications of an illness.

Questions

Q76

LIVID

*Your Own Answer*_____

Q77

COMMODIOUS

*Your Own Answer*_____

Q78

PEREMPTORY

*Your Own Answer*_____

Correct Answers

A76

adj.—discolored, as if bruised; extremely angry; furious

After the fall, her arm was **livid**.

A77

adj.—spacious and convenient; roomy

The new home was so **commodious** that many new pieces of furniture needed to be purchased.

A78

adj.—barring future action; that cannot be denied, changed, etc.

The **peremptory** means of defense was satisfactory to keep out the intruders.

Questions

Q79

PLACATE

*Your Own Answer*_____

Q80

ALCHEMIST

*Your Own Answer*_____

Q81

ADVERSE

*Your Own Answer*_____

Correct Answers

A79

v.—to appease or pacify
The entire family attempted to **placate** the stubborn child.

A80

n.—a person who studies chemistry
The **alchemist's** laboratory was full of bottles and tubes of strange looking liquids.

A81

adj.—negative; hostile; antagonistic; inimical
Contrary to the ski resort's expectations, the warm weather generated **adverse** conditions for a profitable weekend.

Questions

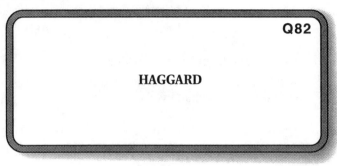

Q82

HAGGARD

*Your Own Answer*_____

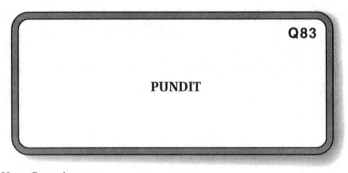

Q83

PUNDIT

*Your Own Answer*_____

Q84

CALIBER

*Your Own Answer*_____

Correct Answers

A82

adj.—untamed; having a worn look

The homeless man had a **haggard** look, reflecting all the years he had lived on the street.

A83

n.—a person claiming to have great knowledge

The university is full of **pundits**.

A84

n.—quality

The **caliber** of talent at the show was excellent.

Questions

GERMANE

*Your Own Answer*_____

STANCH

*Your Own Answer*_____

VERBATIM

*Your Own Answer*_____

Correct Answers

A85

adj.—pertinent; related; to the point

Her essay contained **germane** information, relevant to the new Constitutional amendment.

A86

v.—to stop or check the flow of; to staunch

It is necessary to **stanch** the bleeding from the wound as soon as possible.

A87

adj.—employing the same words as another; literal

He was accused of plagiarism since he repeated **verbatim** what one of his professors had written many years before.

Questions

PERMEABLE

*Your Own Answer*_____

BURNISH

*Your Own Answer*_____

SANGUINE

*Your Own Answer*_____

Correct Answers

A88

adj.—porous; allowing to pass through
Because the material was **permeable**, the water
was able to drain.

A89

v.—to polish by rubbing
The vase needed to be **burnished** to restore its
beauty.

A90

adj.—optimistic; cheerful; red
Even when victory seemed impossible, the
general remained **sanguine**.

Questions

Q91

SPECIOUS

*Your Own Answer*_____

Q92

ROUT

*Your Own Answer*_____

Q93

ANECDOTE

*Your Own Answer*_____

Correct Answers

A91

adj.—plausible, but deceptive; apparently, but not actually true

The jury forewoman said the jury saw through the defense lawyer's **specious** argument and convicted his client on the weight of the evidence.

A92

n.; v.—1. a noisy or disorderly crowd; a retreat or terrible defeat 2. to dig up

1. The **rout** kept the police busy all morning with crowd control.

2. The dog **routed** around for her bone.

A93

n.—a short account of happenings

The speaker told an **anecdote** about how he lost his shoes when he was young.

Questions

Q94

NEMESIS

*Your Own Answer*_____

Q95

REFURBISH

*Your Own Answer*_____

Q96

CONSPICUOUS

*Your Own Answer*_____

Correct Answers

n.—a person who inflicts just punishment; retribution; a rival

The criminal was killed by his **nemesis**, the brother of the man he murdered.

v.—to make new; to renovate

The Newsomes are **refurbishing** their old colonial home with the help of an interior designer.

adj.—easy to see; noticeable

The diligent and hardworking editor thought the obvious mistake was **conspicuous**.

Questions

VALIANT

*Your Own Answer*_____

VITAL

*Your Own Answer*_____

IMPARTIAL

*Your Own Answer*_____

Correct Answers

A97

adj.—full of courage or bravery

The firefighter made a **valiant** effort to save the trapped person.

A98

adj.—important; spirited

When in a foreign country, a passport is a **vital** piece of paperwork to have at all times.

A99

adj.—unbiased; fair

Exasperated by charges to the contrary, the judge reiterated that he had bent over backwards to be **impartial** in a case that crackled with emotion.

Questions

Q100

EXTRICABLE

*Your Own Answer*_____

Q101

REDOLENT

*Your Own Answer*_____

Q102

WRATH

*Your Own Answer*_____

Correct Answers

A100

adj.—capable of being disentangled
The knots were complicated, but **extricable**.

A101

adj.—sweet-smelling; having the odor of a particular thing
The **redolent** aroma of the pie tempted everyone.

A102

n.—violent or unrestrained anger; fury
Do not trespass on his property or you will have to deal with his **wrath**.

Questions

Q103

PENCHANT

*Your Own Answer*_____

Q104

ACCOLADE

*Your Own Answer*_____

Q105

DISSONANT

*Your Own Answer*_____

Correct Answers

A103

n.—a liking for
I have a **penchant** for all flavors of ice cream.

A104

n.—approving or praising mention; a sign of
approval or respect
Rich **accolades** were bestowed on the returning
hero.

A105

adj.—not in harmony; in disagreement
Despite several intense rehearsals, the voices of
the choir members continued to be **dissonant**.

Questions

Q106

CONTIGUOUS

*Your Own Answer*_____

Q107

LECHEROUS

*Your Own Answer*_____

Q108

REPROBATE

*Your Own Answer*_____

Correct Answers

A106

adj.—touching; or adjoining and close, but not touching

There are many **contiguous** buildings in the city because there is no excess land to allow space between them.

A107

adj.—impure in thought and act

The **lecherous** Humbert Humbert is Nabokov's protagonist in *Lolita*, a novel that sparked great controversy because of Humbert's romantic attachment to a young girl.

A108

v.; adj.—1. to condemn; to reject
2. unprincipled; corrupt

1. The teacher will **reprobate** the actions of the delinquent student.
2. The **reprobate** judge was convicted of accepting bribes.

Questions

Q109

REVILE

*Your Own Answer*_____

Q110

EXORBITANT

*Your Own Answer*_____

Q111

STIPEND

*Your Own Answer*_____

Correct Answers

A109

v.—to be abusive in speech

It is not appropriate for a teacher to **revile** a student.

A110

adj.—going beyond what is reasonable; excessive

Paying hundreds of dollars for the dress is an **exorbitant** amount.

A111

n.—payment for work done

She receives a monthly **stipend** for her help with the project.

Questions

Q112

REALM

*Your Own Answer*_____

Q113

IOTA

*Your Own Answer*_____

Q114

AMALGAM

*Your Own Answer*_____

Correct Answers

A112

n.—an area; sphere of activity

In the **realm** of health care, the issue of who pays and how is never far from the surface.

A113

n.—a very small piece

There wasn't one **iota** of evidence to suggest a conspiracy.

A114

n.—a mixture or combination (often of metals)

The art display was an **amalgam** of modern and traditional pieces.

Questions

Q115

RAMPANT

*Your Own Answer*_____

Q116

ASPERSION

*Your Own Answer*_____

Q117

MALEVOLENT

*Your Own Answer*_____

Correct Answers

A115

adj.—growing unchecked; widespread
Social unrest was **rampant** because of the lack of food available to the people.

A116

n.—slanderous statement; a damaging or derogatory criticism
The **aspersion** damaged the credibility of the organization.

A117

adj.—wishing evil (opposite: benevolent)
The man intimidated his opponent with threats and **malevolent** words.

Questions

Q118

ECONOMICAL

*Your Own Answer*_____

Q119

LOITER

*Your Own Answer*_____

Q120

TARRY

*Your Own Answer*_____

Correct Answers

A118

adj.—not wasteful; thrifty

With her **economical** sense she was able to save the company thousands of dollars.

A119

v.—to spend time aimlessly

Many teenagers **loiter** around the mall when there is nothing else to do.

A120

v.—to go or move slowly; to delay

She **tarried** too long, and therefore missed her train.

Questions

QUIXOTIC

*Your Own Answer*_____

FIGMENT

*Your Own Answer*_____

PERUSE

*Your Own Answer*_____

Correct Answers

A121

adj.—foolishly idealistic; romantically idealistic; extravagantly chivalrous

He was popular with the ladies due to his **quixotic** charm.

A122

n.—something made up in the mind

The unicorn on the hill was a **figment** of his imagination.

A123

v.—to read carefully; to study

A vast majority of time was spent **perusing** the possible solution to the dilemma.

Questions

Q124

BRUSQUE

*Your Own Answer*_____

Q125

DEPICT

*Your Own Answer*_____

Q126

INGRATIATE

*Your Own Answer*_____

Correct Answers

A124

adj.—abrupt in manner or speech

His **brusque** answer was neither acceptable nor polite.

A125

v.—to portray; to describe

The mural **depicts** the life of a typical urban dweller.

A126

v.—to bring into one's good graces

The man was hoping to **ingratiate** himself with his wife by buying a bouquet of flowers and candy.

Questions

Q127

FLUENCY

*Your Own Answer*_____

Q128

SAGACIOUS

*Your Own Answer*_____

Q129

PARAPET

*Your Own Answer*_____

Correct Answers

A127

n.—ability to speak easily and expressively
The child's **fluency** in Spanish and English was
remarkable.

A128

adj.—wise
Many of her friends came to her with their
problems because she gave **sagacious** advice.

A129

n.—a wall for protection; a low wall or railing
The **parapet** protected the kingdom from the
raging army.

Questions

Q130

PERNICIOUS

*Your Own Answer*_____

Q131

SUNDRY

*Your Own Answer*_____

Q132

REPROOF

*Your Own Answer*_____

Correct Answers

A130

adj.—dangerous; harmful

A snowstorm or heavy rains can have a **pernicious** impact on a driver's control of the road.

A131

adj.—various; miscellaneous; separate; distinct

This store sells many **sundry** novelty items.

A132

n.—a rebuke

For all his hard work, all he got was a **reproof** of his efforts.

Questions

Q133

RHETORICAL

Your Own Answer

Q134

INTRACTABLE

Your Own Answer

Q135

PARADIGM

Your Own Answer

Correct Answers

A133

adj.—having to do with verbal communication; having to do with a question asked merely for effect with no answer expected

In posing a **rhetorical** question, he hoped to get people thinking.

A134

adj.—stubborn, obstinate; not easily taught or disciplined

Every teacher in the school became frustrated with the **intractable** student and sent him to the principal's office.

A135

n.—model; prototype; pattern

The machine could no longer be produced after the **paradigm** was destroyed.

Questions

Q136

LIGNEOUS

*Your Own Answer*_____

Q137

UNOBTRUSIVE

*Your Own Answer*_____

Q138

CLEMENCY

*Your Own Answer*_____

Correct Answers

A136

adj.—having the composition of wood
The **ligneous** material appeared to be pure oak.

A137

adj.—out of the way; remaining quietly in the background
The shy man found an **unobtrusive** seat in the far corner of the room.

A138

n.—mercy toward an offender; mildness
The governor granted the prisoner **clemency**.

Questions

CACOPHONY

*Your Own Answer*_____

SUFFUSE

*Your Own Answer*_____

MIRE

*Your Own Answer*_____

Correct Answers

A139

n.—a harsh, inharmonious collection of sounds; dissonance

The beautiful harmony of the symphony was well enjoyed after the **cacophony** coming from the stage as the orchestra warmed up.

A140

v.—to overspread

The rain will **suffuse** the spilled sand around the patio.

A141

v.—to cause to get stuck in wet, soggy ground

The car became **mired** in the mud.

Questions

Q142

QUAFF

*Your Own Answer*_____

Q143

PULCHRITUDE

*Your Own Answer*_____

Q144

CONVENTIONAL

*Your Own Answer*_____

Correct Answers

A142

v.—to drink deeply
A dog will **quaff** if he becomes overheated.

A143

n.—beauty
The **pulchritude** of the girl is seen in her bright smile.

A144

adj.—traditional; common; routine
The bride wanted a **conventional** wedding ceremony, complete with a white dress, many flowers, and a grand reception party.

Questions

BETROTH

*Your Own Answer*_____

DESTITUTE

*Your Own Answer*_____

VIRTUOSO

*Your Own Answer*_____

Correct Answers

A145

v.—to promise or pledge in marriage
The man **betrothed** his daughter to the prince.

A146

adj.—poor; poverty-stricken
One Bangladeshi bank makes loans to **destitute** citizens so that they may overcome their poverty.

A147

n.—highly skilled artist
The **virtuoso** played piano with the best orchestras in the world.

Questions

Q148

LAX

*Your Own Answer*_____

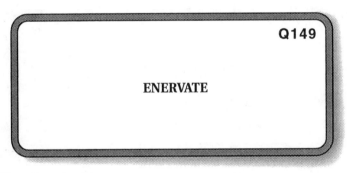

Q149

ENERVATE

*Your Own Answer*_____

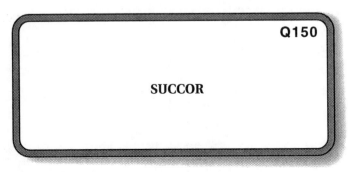

Q150

SUCCOR

*Your Own Answer*_____

Correct Answers

adj.—careless; irresponsible

She was **lax** in everything she did and therefore could not be trusted with important tasks.

v.—to weaken; to deprive of nerve or strength

The sickness **enervates** its victims until they can no longer get out of bed.

n.—aid; assistance

Succor was given to the fire victim in the form of clothes and temporary shelter.

Questions

Q151

INCOMMODIOUS

*Your Own Answer*_____

Q152

CHAFE

*Your Own Answer*_____

Q153

RETROACTION

*Your Own Answer*_____

Correct Answers

A151

adj.—inconvenient
The **incommodious** illness caused her to miss
an important interview.

A152

v.—to annoy, to irritate; to wear away or make
sore by rubbing
His constant teasing **chafed** her.

A153

n.—a reverse action
The **retroaction** of the car sent those standing
behind it fleeing.

Questions

Q154

HUMILITY

*Your Own Answer*_____

Q155

VEHEMENT

*Your Own Answer*_____

Q156

MITIGATE

*Your Own Answer*_____

Correct Answers

A154

n.—lack of pride; modesty
Full of **humility**, she accepted the award but
gave all the credit to her mentor.

A155

adj.—using great force; described by strong
feelings
After trying for hours, his **vehement** efforts
finally yielded some positive results.

A156

v.—to alleviate; to lessen; to soothe
She tried to **mitigate** the loss of his pet by
buying him a kitten.

Questions

Q157

SALUBRIOUS

*Your Own Answer*_____

Q158

FACTION

*Your Own Answer*_____

Q159

SURPASS

*Your Own Answer*_____

Correct Answers

adj.—promoting good health
Salubrious food helps maintain an ideal weight.

n.—a number of people in an organization working for a common cause against the main body
A **faction** of the student body supported the president's view.

v.—to go beyond; outdo
After recovering from a serious illness, the boy **surpassed** the doctor's expectations by leaving the hospital two days early.

Questions

Q160

CIRCUMLOCUTION

*Your Own Answer*_____

Q161

TEMERITY

*Your Own Answer*_____

Q162

DESULTORY

*Your Own Answer*_____

Correct Answers

A160

n.—a roundabout or indirect way of speaking; not to the point

The man's speech contained so much **circumlocution** that I was unsure of the point he was trying to make.

A161

n.—foolhardiness

Temerity can result in tragedy if the activity is dangerous.

A162

adj.—moving in a random, directionless manner

The thefts were occurring in a **desultory** manner making them difficult to track.

Questions

Q163

DERISIVE

*Your Own Answer*_____

Q164

METAMORPHOSIS

*Your Own Answer*_____

Q165

IMPENITENT

*Your Own Answer*_____

Correct Answers

A163

adj.—showing disrespect or scorn for

The **derisive** comment was aimed at the man's lifelong enemy.

A164

n.—change of form

A **metamorphosis** caused the caterpillar to become a beautiful butterfly.

A165

adj.—without regret, shame, or remorse

It was obvious after his **impenitent** remark to the press that the defendant felt no remorse for his crime.

Questions

Q166

QUALIFIED

*Your Own Answer*_____

Q167

EFFUSIVE

*Your Own Answer*_____

Q168

INUNDATE

*Your Own Answer*_____

Correct Answers

A166

adj.—experienced; limited or modified in some way

She was well **qualified** for the job after working in the field for ten years.

A167

adj.—pouring out or forth; overflowing

The **effusive** currents rush through the broken dam.

A168

v.—to flood; to overwhelm with a large amount of

The broken water main **inundated** the business district with water.

Questions

Q169

CHARLATAN

Your Own Answer

Q170

GARRULOUS

Your Own Answer

Q171

SERENDIPITY

Your Own Answer

Correct Answers

A169

n.—a person who pretends to have knowledge; an impostor; a fake

The **charlatan** deceived the townspeople.

A170

adj.—extremely talkative or wordy

No one wanted to speak with the **garrulous** man for fear of being stuck in a long, one-sided conversation.

A171

n.—an apparent aptitude for making fortunate discoveries accidentally

Serendipity seemed to follow the lucky winner wherever he went.

Questions

Q172

JADED

*Your Own Answer*_____

Q173

PURLOIN

*Your Own Answer*_____

Q174

QUIESCENCE

*Your Own Answer*_____

Correct Answers

A172

adj.—worn-out

A person may become **jaded** if forced to work too many hours.

A173

v.—to take wrongfully; to steal

It is unethical to **purloin** things which do not belong to oneself.

A174

n.—state of being at rest or without motion

After a tough day on the shipping dock, one needs **quiescence**.

Questions

Q175

FERVID

*Your Own Answer*_____

Q176

GULLIBLE

*Your Own Answer*_____

Q177

VIGOR

*Your Own Answer*_____

Correct Answers

A175

adj.—intensely hot; fervent; impassioned

Her **fervid** skin alerted the doctor to her fever.

A176

adj.—easily fooled

Gullible people are vulnerable to practical jokes.

A177

n.—energy; forcefulness

He took on the task with great **vigor**, proving his doubters wrong.

Questions

Q178

FEASIBLE

*Your Own Answer*_____

Q179

CHARY

*Your Own Answer*_____

Q180

EXTOL

*Your Own Answer*_____

Correct Answers

A178

adj.—reasonable; practical
Increased exercise is a **feasible** means of weight loss.

A179

adj.—cautious; being sparing in giving
Be **chary** when driving at night.

A180

v.—to give great praise
The father will **extol** the success of his son to everyone he meets.

Questions

Q181

CITADEL

*Your Own Answer*_____

Q182

DISCRETE

*Your Own Answer*_____

Q183

FLAGRANT

*Your Own Answer*_____

Correct Answers

A181

n.—a fortress set up high to defend a city

A **citadel** sat on the hill to protect the city below.

A182

adj.—separate; individually distinct; composed of distinct parts

There were four **discrete** aspects to the architecture of the home.

A183

adj.—glaringly wrong

The **flagrant** foul was apparent to everyone.

Questions

Q184

HALCYON

*Your Own Answer*_____

Q185

CAPRICIOUS

*Your Own Answer*_____

Q186

SLANDER

*Your Own Answer*_____

Correct Answers

A184

adj.—tranquil; happy

The old man fondly remembered his **halcyon** days growing up on the farm.

A185

adj.—changeable; fickle

The **capricious** bride-to-be has a different church in mind for her wedding every few days.

A186

v.—to defame; to maliciously misrepresent

Orville said he'd been **slandered**, and he asked the court who would—or could—give him his name back.

Questions

PLATONIC

*Your Own Answer*_____

WITHER

*Your Own Answer*_____

NUGATORY

*Your Own Answer*_____

Correct Answers

adj.—idealistic or impractical; not amorous or sensual

The **platonic** relationship between John and Cybil caused much stress to John's marriage.

v.—to wilt; to shrivel; to humiliate; to cut down

The plant **withered** slowly since it received little light and little water.

adj.—trifling; futile; insignificant

Because the problem was **nugatory** it was not addressed immediately.

Questions

Q190

BOOR

*Your Own Answer*_____

Q191

IMPUTATION

*Your Own Answer*_____

Q192

ASTUTE

*Your Own Answer*_____

Correct Answers

A190

n.—a rude person

The **boor** was not invited to the party, but he came anyway.

A191

n.—the act of charging or attributing a fault or misconduct to another

The **imputation** of guilt was made by the judge.

A192

adj.—cunning; sly; crafty

The **astute** lawyer's questioning convinced the jury of the defendant's guilt.

Questions

Q193

JOVIAL

*Your Own Answer*_____

Q194

WINSOME

*Your Own Answer*_____

Q195

SPURN

*Your Own Answer*_____

Correct Answers

A193

adj.—cheery; jolly; playful

She was a **jovial** person, always pleasant and fun to be with.

A194

adj.—charming; sweetly attractive

His **winsome** words moved the crowd to love him even more.

A195

v.; n.—1. to push away 2. a strong rejection

1. The woman **spurned** the advances of her suitor, saying she wasn't ready for a commitment.

2. Unlucky enough to be the ninth telemarketer to call Jane that evening, he caught her **spurn**.

Questions

Q196

JOLLITY

*Your Own Answer*_____

Q197

PERCUSSION

*Your Own Answer*_____

Q198

OBSTINATE

*Your Own Answer*_____

Correct Answers

A196

n.—the quality or state of being fun or jolly

The **jollity** of the crowd was seen in the cheering and laughing.

A197

n.—striking one object against another

The loud **percussion** of the hunter's gunshot startled the birds.

A198

adj.—stubborn

Her father would not allow her to stay out past midnight; she thought he was **obstinate** because he would not change his mind.

Questions

Q199

DESIST

*Your Own Answer*_____

Q200

EMBARKATION

*Your Own Answer*_____

Q201

IDYLL

*Your Own Answer*_____

Correct Answers

A199

v.—to stop or cease

The judge ordered the man to **desist** from calling his ex-wife in the middle of the night.

A200

n.—the act of engaging or investing in an enterprise or journey

The clerk approved the committee's **embarkation** into the field of education.

A201

n.–a written piece of work describing a peaceful rural scene

Reading the **idyll** made me think of the family farm.

Questions

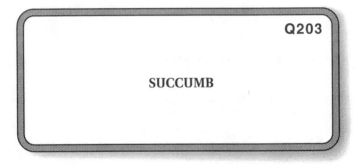

Q202

TABLE

*Your Own Answer*_____

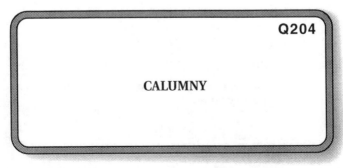

Q203

SUCCUMB

*Your Own Answer*_____

Q204

CALUMNY

*Your Own Answer*_____

Correct Answers

A202

n.; v.—1. a systematic list of details 2. to make a list

1. The train schedule was set up as a **table**.
2. The porter **tabled** the inventory of luggage.

A203

v.—to give in; to yield; to collapse

When dieting, it is difficult not to **succumb** to temptation.

A204

n.—slander

I felt it necessary to speak against the **calumny** of the man's good reputation.

Questions

CASCADE

*Your Own Answer*_____

UNGAINLY

*Your Own Answer*_____

DISPARITY

*Your Own Answer*_____

Correct Answers

A205

n; v.—1. waterfall 2. to pour; to rush; to fall

1. The hikers stopped along the path to take in the beauty of the rushing **cascade**.

2. The water **cascaded** down the rocks into the pool.

A206

adj.—clumsy and unattractive

The **ungainly** man knocked over the plant stand.

A207

n.—difference in form, character, or degree

There is a great **disparity** between a light snack and a great feast.

Questions

Q208

BATTEN

*Your Own Answer*_____

Q209

ENGENDER

*Your Own Answer*_____

Q210

QUIRK

*Your Own Answer*_____

Correct Answers

A208

n.; v.—1. a strip of wood or steel used to fasten or cover an opening 2. to fasten or strengthen with battens

1. The sailors used the **battens** to hold the canvas over the hatchway.
2. The captain ordered all hatches **battened**.

A209

v.—to bring about; to beget; to bring forth

The group attempted to **engender** changes to the law.

A210

n.—peculiar behavior; startling twist

Nobody's perfect—we all have our **quirks**.

Questions

Q211

PROFUSION

*Your Own Answer*_____

Q212

KNEAD

*Your Own Answer*_____

Q213

REGAL

*Your Own Answer*_____

Correct Answers

A211

n.—great wastefulness; a large abundance of

The **profusion** of the food fight was unforgivable considering the worldwide hunger problem.

A212

v.—mix; massage

After mixing the ingredients, they **kneaded** the dough and set it aside to rise.

A213

adj.—royal; grand

The **regal** home was lavishly decorated and furnished with European antiques.

Questions

Q214

HARANGUE

*Your Own Answer*_____

Q215

DILIGENCE

*Your Own Answer*_____

Q216

INDECIPHERABLE

*Your Own Answer*_____

Correct Answers

n; v.—1. a lengthy, heartfelt speech 2. to talk or write excitedly

1. We sat patiently and listened to her **harangue**.

2. When he finally stopped his **haranguing**, I responded calmly.

n.—hard work

Anything can be accomplished with **diligence** and commitment.

adj.—illegible

The scribbling on the paper is **indecipherable**.

Questions

VIABLE

*Your Own Answer*_____

EFFACE

*Your Own Answer*_____

SQUALID

*Your Own Answer*_____

Correct Answers

adj.—capable of maintaining life; possible; attainable

Is life **viable** on Mars?

v.—to erase; to make inconspicuous

Hiding in the woods, the soldier was **effaced** by his camouflage uniform.

adj.—filthy; wretched (from squalor)

The lack of sanitation piping caused **squalid** conditions.

Questions

Q220

VACUOUS

*Your Own Answer*_____

Q221

ILLUMINATE

*Your Own Answer*_____

Q222

CHORTLE

*Your Own Answer*_____

Correct Answers

adj.—dull, stupid; empty-headed

For a time, viewers of TV's *Murphy Brown* looked forward to the seemingly unending parade of **vacuous** secretaries that Murphy went through.

v.—to make understandable

I asked a classmate to **illuminate** the professor's far-ranging lecture for me.

v.; n.—1. to make a gleeful, chuckling sound 2. a sound like a chuckle

1. The small man **chortled** at the sight of the giant stuck in the chair.
2. The **chortle** coming from the horse caught everyone by surprise.

Questions

Q223

EMBELLISH

*Your Own Answer*_____

Q224

DEBASE

*Your Own Answer*_____

Q225

FERRET

*Your Own Answer*_____

Correct Answers

v.—to improve by adding details
Adding beads to a garment will **embellish** it.

v.—to make lower in quality
The French are concerned that Franglais, a blending of English and French, will **debase** their language.

v.; n.—1. to force out of hiding; to search for
2. a small, weasel-like mammal

1. The police will **ferret** the fugitive out of his hiding place.

2. I spent the morning **ferreting** for my keys.

Questions

Q226

CLOYING

*Your Own Answer*_____

Q227

DEFUNCT

*Your Own Answer*_____

Q228

DISHEARTENED

*Your Own Answer*_____

Correct Answers

A226

adj.—too sugary; too sentimental or flattering

After years of marriage, the husband still gave **cloying** gifts to his wife.

A227

adj.—no longer living or existing

The man lost a large sum of money when the company went **defunct**.

A228

adj.—discouraged; depressed

After failing the exam, the student became **disheartened** and wondered if he would ever graduate.

Questions

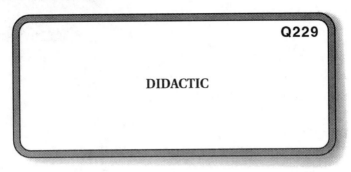

Q229

DIDACTIC

*Your Own Answer*_____

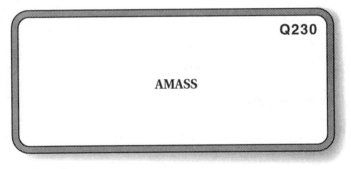

Q230

AMASS

*Your Own Answer*_____

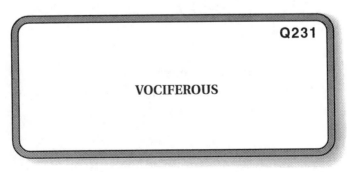

Q231

VOCIFEROUS

*Your Own Answer*_____

Correct Answers

A229

adj.—instructive; dogmatic; preachy
Our teacher's **didactic** technique boosted our scores.

A230

v.—to collect together; to accumulate
Over the years the sailor has **amassed** many replicas of boats.

A231

adj.—making a loud outcry
Vociferous noises emerged from the dark cave.

Questions

EPILOGUE

*Your Own Answer*_____

FRET

*Your Own Answer*_____

MAGNANIMITY

*Your Own Answer*_____

Correct Answers

A232

n.—closing section of a play or novel providing further comment

The **epilogue** told us the destiny of the characters.

A233

v.—to make rough or disturb

The pet will **fret** the floor if he continues to scratch.

A234

n.—a quality of nobleness of mind, disdain of meanness or revenge

Being full of **magnanimity** he asked the thief only for an apology and set him free.

Questions

Q235

ELUCIDATE

*Your Own Answer*_____

Q236

PRODIGIOUS

*Your Own Answer*_____

Q237

AVARICE

*Your Own Answer*_____

Correct Answers

A235

v.—to make clear; to explain

In the paper's conclusion, its purpose was **elucidated** in one sentence.

A236

adj.—wonderful; enormous

The **prodigious** festivities lasted until the wee hours of the morning.

A237

n.—inordinate desire for gaining and possessing wealth

The man's **avarice** for money kept him at work through the evenings and weekends.

Questions

HYPOCRITICAL

*Your Own Answer*_____

GLUTTON

*Your Own Answer*_____

INDULGENT

*Your Own Answer*_____

Correct Answers

A238

adj.—two-faced; deceptive

His constituents believed that the governor was **hypocritical** for calling for a moratorium on negative campaigning while continuing to air some of the most vicious ads ever produced against his opponent.

A239

n.—overeater

The **glutton** ate 12 hot dogs in an hour.

A240

adj.—kind or lenient, often to excess

He was being **indulgent** when he bought both a pony and a bicycle for his daughter's birthday.

Questions

Q241

INEPT

*Your Own Answer*_____

Q242

PRECOCIOUS

*Your Own Answer*_____

Q243

DELIQUESCE

*Your Own Answer*_____

Correct Answers

A241

adj.—incompetent; clumsy

She would rather update the budget book herself, since her assistant is so **inept**.

A242

adj.—developed or matured earlier than usual

The **precocious** eight-year-old wanted to read the romance novel.

A243

v.—to dissolve

The snow **deliquesced** when the temperature rose.

Questions

Q244

ABANDON

*Your Own Answer*_____

Q245

FACILITATE

*Your Own Answer*_____

Q246

PASSIVE

*Your Own Answer*_____

Correct Answers

A244

v.; n.—1. to leave behind; to give something up
2. freedom; enthusiasm; impetuosity

1. After failing for several years, he **abandoned** his dream of starting a grocery business.

2. Lucy embarked on her new adventure with **abandon**.

A245

v.—to make easier; to simplify

The new ramp by the door's entrance **facilitated** access to the building for those in wheelchairs.

A246

adj.—submissive; unassertive

He is so **passive** that others walk all over him.

Questions

ASPIRANT

*Your Own Answer*_____

BENEFICENT

*Your Own Answer*_____

SOLEMNITY

*Your Own Answer*_____

Correct Answers

n.—a person who goes after high goals

The **aspirant** would not settle for assistant director—only the top job was good enough.

adj.—conferring benefits; kindly; doing good

He is a **beneficent** person, always taking in stray animals and talking to people who need someone to listen.

n.—a deep, reverent feeling often associated with religious occasions

The church service was full of **solemnity**.

Questions

Q250

BENIGN

*Your Own Answer*_____

Q251

TRANSMUTATION

*Your Own Answer*_____

Q252

ASTRINGENT

*Your Own Answer*_____

Correct Answers

A250

adj.—mild; harmless

A lamb is a **benign** animal, especially when compared with a lion.

A251

n.—a changed form

Somewhere in the network's entertainment division, the show underwent a **transmutation** from a half-hour sitcom into an hour-long drama.

A252

n.; adj.—1. a substance that contracts bodily tissues causing contraction, tightening 2. stern, austere

1. After the operation an **astringent** was used on his skin so that the stretched area would return to normal.

2. The downturn in sales caused the CEO to impose **astringent** measures.

Questions

Q253

AUSTERE

*Your Own Answer*_____

Q254

IRONIC

*Your Own Answer*_____

Q255

ORNATE

*Your Own Answer*_____

Correct Answers

A253

adj.—having a stern look; having strict self-discipline

The old woman always has an **austere** look about her.

A254

adj.—contradictory, inconsistent; sarcastic

Is it not **ironic** that Americans will toss out leftover french fries while people around the globe continue to starve?

A255

adj.—elaborate; lavish; decorated

The courthouse was framed by **ornate** friezes.

Questions

Q256

CATACLYSM

*Your Own Answer*_____

Q257

PHLEGMATIC

*Your Own Answer*_____

Q258

DEMUR

*Your Own Answer*_____

Correct Answers

A256

n.—an extreme natural force

The earthquake has been the first **cataclysm** in five years.

A257

adj.—without emotion or interest; sluggish and dull

The playwright had hoped his story would take theatergoers on an emotional roller coaster, but on opening night they just sat there, stone-faced and **phlegmatic**.

A258

v.; n.—1. to object 2. objection; misgiving

1. She hated animals, so when the subject of buying a cat came up, she **demurred**.

2. She said yes, but he detected a **demur** in her voice.

Questions

ENCOMIUM

*Your Own Answer*_____

GAUNTLET

*Your Own Answer*_____

LUCID

*Your Own Answer*_____

Correct Answers

A259

n.—formal expression of high praise

The sitcom actress gave her costars a long **encomium** as she accepted her Emmy.

A260

n.—a protective glove

The **gauntlet** saved the man's hand from being burned in the fire.

A261

adj.—shiny; clear-minded

He chose a shimmering, **lucid** fabric for his curtains.

Questions

Q262

TIMOROUS

Your Own Answer

Q263

CONFLUENCE

Your Own Answer

Q264

HINDRANCE

Your Own Answer

Correct Answers

A262

adj.—lacking courage; timid
The **timorous** child hid behind his parents.

A263

n.—a thing that is joined together
Great cities often lie at the **confluence** of great rivers.

A264

n.—blockage; obstacle
His assistance often seems to be more of a **hindrance** than a help.

Questions

Q265

DINT

*Your Own Answer*_____

Q266

GARBLED

*Your Own Answer*_____

Q267

MERETRICIOUS

*Your Own Answer*_____

Correct Answers

A265

n.—strength

The **dint** of the bridge could hold trucks weighing many tons.

A266

adj.—mixed up; distorted or confused

The interference on the phone line caused the data to become **garbled** on the computer screen.

A267

adj.—deceptive beauty; alluring by falsely attractive appearance; characteristics of a prostitute

A cubic zirconia is a **meretricious** way of impressing others.

Questions

SOLACE

*Your Own Answer*_____

OPPROBRIOUS

*Your Own Answer*_____

INFAMY

*Your Own Answer*_____

Correct Answers

A268

n.—hope; comfort during a time of grief

When her father passed away, she found **solace** amongst her friends and family.

A269

adj.—abusive

Nobody liked working for him because he was so **opprobrious**.

A270

n.—a bad reputation

The town had only 98 residents, so all it took was one bad apple to bring **infamy** on the whole place.

Questions

TRANSMUTE

*Your Own Answer*_____

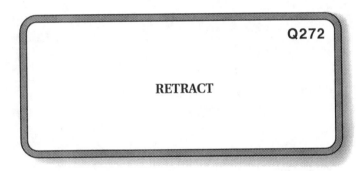

RETRACT

*Your Own Answer*_____

SAVOR

*Your Own Answer*_____

Correct Answers

A271

v.—to transform

Decorators **transmute** ordinary homes into interesting showcases.

A272

v.—to draw or take back

Once you say something, it's hard to **retract**.

A273

v.—to receive pleasure from; to enjoy with appreciation; to dwell on with delight

After several months without a day off, she **savored** every minute of her week-long vacation.

Questions

COPIOUS

*Your Own Answer*_____

ALACRITY

*Your Own Answer*_____

INGRATITUDE

*Your Own Answer*_____

Correct Answers

A274

adj.—abundant; in great quantities

Her **copious** notes touched on every subject presented in the lecture.

A275

n.—eager readiness or speed

The manager was so impressed by the worker's **alacrity** he suggested a promotion.

A276

n.—ungratefulness

When she failed to send a thank-you card, her friend took it as a sign of **ingratitude**.

Questions

PRAGMATIC

*Your Own Answer*_____

EON

*Your Own Answer*_____

POTENT

*Your Own Answer*_____

Correct Answers

adj.—matter-of-fact; practical
Since they were saving money to buy a new home, the **pragmatic** married couple decided not to go on an expensive vacation.

n.—an indefinitely long period of time
The star may have existed for **eons**.

adj.—having great power or physical strength
He took very **potent** medication and felt better immediately.

Questions

Q280

DURESS

*Your Own Answer*_____

Q281

PRECARIOUS

*Your Own Answer*_____

Q282

FISSURE

*Your Own Answer*_____

Correct Answers

A280

n.—imprisonment; the use of threats

His **duress** was supposed to last 10–15 years.

A281

adj.—depending upon another; risky, uncertain

The **precarious** plans fell through when the second couple changed their plans.

A282

n.—a cleft or crack

The earthquake caused a **fissure** that split the cliff face.

Questions

Q283

DERIDE

*Your Own Answer*_____

Q284

EFFEMINATE

*Your Own Answer*_____

Q285

AESTHETIC

*Your Own Answer*_____

Correct Answers

A283

v.—to laugh at with contempt; to mock
No matter what he said, he was **derided**.

A284

adj.—having qualities attributed to a woman;
delicate
A high-pitched laugh made the man seem
effeminate.

A285

adj.—of beauty; pertaining to taste in art and
beauty
She found that her **aesthetic** sense and that of
the artist were at odds.

Questions

Q286

ABEYANCE

*Your Own Answer*_____

Q287

IMPLICIT

*Your Own Answer*_____

Q288

TURMOIL

*Your Own Answer*_____

Correct Answers

A286

n.—a state of temporary suspension or inactivity

Since the power failure, the town has been in **abeyance**.

A287

adj.—understood but not plainly stated; without doubt

The child's anger was **implicit**.

A288

n.—unrest; agitation

Before the country recovered after the war, they experienced a time of great **turmoil**.

Questions

Q289

AROMATIC

Your Own Answer

Q290

ENFEEBLE

Your Own Answer

Q291

CONSEQUENTIAL

Your Own Answer

Correct Answers

A289

adj.—having a smell that is sweet or spicy
The **aromatic** smell coming from the oven
made the man's mouth water.

A290

v.—to make weak
The illness will **enfeeble** anyone who catches it.

A291

adj.—following as an effect; important
His long illness and **consequential** absence set
him behind in his homework.

Questions

Q292

SCRUPULOUS

*Your Own Answer*_____

Q293

PROBITY

*Your Own Answer*_____

Q294

VAGABOND

*Your Own Answer*_____

Correct Answers

A292

adj.—honorable; exact

After finding a purse with valuable items inside, the **scrupulous** Mr. Prendergast returned everything to its owner.

A293

n.—honesty

The young man's **probity** was reassuring to the fearful parent.

A294

n.—wanderer; one without a fixed place

Sam was the kind of **vagabond** who enjoyed hitching a ride on a freight train just to see where it would take him.

Questions

Q295

ALLOCATE

*Your Own Answer*_____

Q296

EXPEDITE

*Your Own Answer*_____

Q297

DISSEMBLE

*Your Own Answer*_____

Correct Answers

A295

v.—to set aside; to designate; to assign

There have been front row seats **allocated** to the performer's family.

A296

v.—to hasten the action of

We can **expedite** the bank transaction if we tell them it is an emergency.

A297

v.—to pretend; to feign; to conceal by pretense

The man **dissembled** his assets shamelessly to avoid paying alimony.

Questions

Q298

FORENSIC

*Your Own Answer*_____

Q299

APOCRYPHAL

*Your Own Answer*_____

Q300

PARADOX

*Your Own Answer*_____

Correct Answers

A298

adj.—pertaining to legal or public argument

The **forensic** squad dealt with the legal investigation.

A299

adj.—counterfeit; of doubtful authorship or authenticity

The manuscript supposedly written by Shakespeare had an **apocryphal** quality about it.

A300

n.—a tenet seemingly contradictory or false, but actually true

The **paradox** seemed so unlikely though it was true.

Questions

SPURIOUS

*Your Own Answer*_____

UTOPIA

*Your Own Answer*_____

MUNDANE

*Your Own Answer*_____

Correct Answers

A301

adj.—not genuine, false; bogus
Spurious claims by the importer hid the fact
that prison labor had been used in the gar-
ments' fabrication.

A302

n.—imaginary land with perfect social and
political systems
Voltaire wrote of a **utopia** where the streets were
paved with gold.

A303

adj.—ordinary; commonplace
The small town was very **mundane**.

Questions

Q304

SUPERFICIAL

Your Own Answer

Q305

LUGUBRIOUS

Your Own Answer

Q306

RELEVANT

Your Own Answer

Correct Answers

A304

adj.—on the surface, narrow minded; lacking depth

The victim had two stab wounds, but luckily they were only **superficial**.

A305

adj.—full of sorrow; mournful

The man's **lugubrious** heart kept him from enjoying the special occasion.

A306

adj.—of concern; significant

Asking applicants about their general health is **relevant** since much of the job requires physical strength.

Questions

Q307

ASKANCE

*Your Own Answer*_____

Q308

RETICENT

*Your Own Answer*_____

Q309

INQUISITIVE

*Your Own Answer*_____

Correct Answers

A307

adv.—with a sideways glance of disapproval or suspicion

The guard's **askance** look proved that he suspected them of wrongdoing.

A308

adj.—silent; reserved; shy

The **reticent** girl played with her building blocks while the other children played tag.

A309

adj.—eager to ask questions in order to learn

An **inquisitive** youngster is likely to become a wise adult.

Questions

Q310

CALAMITY

*Your Own Answer*_____

Q311

MAR

*Your Own Answer*_____

Q312

AUTHENTIC

*Your Own Answer*_____

Correct Answers

A310

n.—disaster
The fire in the apartment building was a great **calamity**.

A311

v.—to damage
The statue was **marred** by the ravages of time.

A312

adj.—real; genuine; trustworthy
An **authentic** diamond will cut glass.

Questions

Q313

INADVERTENT

*Your Own Answer*_____

Q314

IGNEOUS

*Your Own Answer*_____

Q315

EARTHY

*Your Own Answer*_____

Correct Answers

A313

adj.—not on purpose; unintentional

It was an **inadvertent** error, to be sure, but nonetheless a mistake that required correction.

A314

adj.—having the nature of fire; volcanic

When the sun shone upon it, the material took on an **igneous** quality.

A315

adj.—unrefined; coarse; simple and natural

The room had an **earthy** quality that reminded him of the outdoors.

Questions

Q316

PROPAGATE

*Your Own Answer*_____

Q317

VESTIGE

*Your Own Answer*_____

Q318

REVERIE

*Your Own Answer*_____

Correct Answers

A316

v.—to reproduce or multiply
Rabbits and gerbils are said to **propagate** quickly.

A317

n.—a trace of something that no longer exists
A **vestige** of scent remained from the flower arrangement.

A318

n.—the condition of being unaware of one's surroundings, trance; dreamy thinking or imagining, especially of agreeable things

As their anniversary neared, Liane fell into a **reverie** as she recalled all the good times she and Roscoe had had.

Questions

VOLUBLE

*Your Own Answer*_____

INCULCATE

*Your Own Answer*_____

TAWDRY

*Your Own Answer*_____

Correct Answers

A319

adj.—fluent; characterized by a great flow of words (talkative)

The **voluble** host barely let his guests get a word in edgewise.

A320

v.—to impress upon the mind, as by insistent urging

I will **inculcate** the directions if people are unsure of them.

A321

adj.—tastelessly ornamented

The shop was full of **tawdry** jewelry.

Questions

LASCIVIOUS

*Your Own Answer*_____

RAZE

*Your Own Answer*_____

INURED

*Your Own Answer*_____

Correct Answers

A322

adj.—indecent; immoral; involves lust

He said it was a harmless pinup poster, but his mother called it **lascivious**.

A323

v.—to scrape or shave off; to obliterate or tear down completely

The plow will **raze** the ice from the road surface.

A324

adj.—accustomed to pain

Beekeepers eventually become **inured** to beestings.

Questions

REPLETE

*Your Own Answer*_____

FLIPPANT

*Your Own Answer*_____

VICARIOUS

*Your Own Answer*_____

Correct Answers

A325

adj.—well-supplied
The kitchen came **replete** with food and utensils.

A326

adj.—talkative; disrespectful
The youngsters were **flippant** in the restaurant.

A327

adj.—done or sacrificed for others
The mother was willing to undergo the **vicarious** surgery for her child.

Questions

Q328

PROMONTORY

Your Own Answer

Q329

SUBSIDIARY

Your Own Answer

Q330

EMOLLIENT

Your Own Answer

Correct Answers

A328

n.—a piece of land jutting into a body of water

The boat hit the rocky **promontory**, splitting the bow.

A329

adj.—giving a service; being in a subordinate position

The function of the **subsidiary** was to oversee the bank's commercial loans.

A330

adj.; n.—1. softening or soothing to the skin; having power to soften or relax living tissues
2. something with a softening or smoothing effect

1. When hands become dry, it may be necessary to soothe them with an **emollient** lotion.
2. The **emollient** did wonders for her chapped lips.

Questions

Q331

INTRANSIGENT

*Your Own Answer*_____

Q332

ETHNIC

*Your Own Answer*_____

Q333

USURPATION

*Your Own Answer*_____

Correct Answers

A331

adj.—uncompromising

No amount of arguing could change her mind because she had **intransigent** values.

A332

adj.—pertaining to races or peoples and their origin, classification, or characteristics

Ethnic foods from five continents were set up on the table.

A333

n.—the act of taking something for oneself; seizure

During the war, the **usurpation** of the country forced an entirely new culture on the natives.

Questions

Q334

BRINDLED

*Your Own Answer*_____

Q335

BREADTH

*Your Own Answer*_____

Q336

INCOMPETENCE

*Your Own Answer*_____

Correct Answers

A334

adj.—mixed with a darker color
In order to get matching paint, we made a **brindled** mixture.

A335

n.—the distance from one side to another
The tablecloth was too small to cover the **breadth** of the table.

A336

n.—failure to meet necessary requirements
The alleged **incompetence** of the construction crew would later become the subject of a class-action suit.

Questions

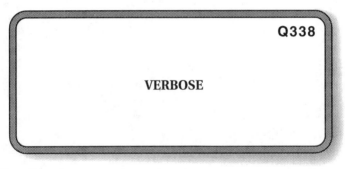

Q337

SOLICIT

*Your Own Answer*_____

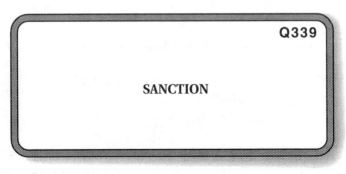

Q338

VERBOSE

*Your Own Answer*_____

Q339

SANCTION

*Your Own Answer*_____

Correct Answers

A337

v.—to ask; to seek

The jobless man **solicited** employment from many factories before he was able to find work.

A338

adj.—wordy; talkative

The **verbose** speech was too long and difficult to follow.

A339

v.; n.—1. to give encouragement; an act of giving authoritative permission 2. a blockade

1. The government has **sanctioned** the meetings as a worthy cause.

2. The **sanctions** did nothing to stop him from seeing his daughter.

Questions

Q340

PROLIFERATE

*Your Own Answer*_____

Q341

UNPRETENTIOUS

*Your Own Answer*_____

Q342

TACIT

*Your Own Answer*_____

Correct Answers

A340

v.—to reproduce quickly

Gerbils are known to be **proliferate** in their reproduction.

A341

adj.—simple; plain; modest

He was an **unpretentious** farmer: an old John Deere and a beat-up Ford pickup were all he needed to get the job done.

A342

adj.—not voiced or expressed

The National Security Agency aide argued, in effect, that he had received the president's **tacit** approval for the arms-for-hostages deal.

Questions

Q343

INEVITABLE

*Your Own Answer*_____

_____

Q344

EXIGENT

*Your Own Answer*_____

_____

Q345

DISTANT

*Your Own Answer*_____

_____

Correct Answers

A343

adj.—sure to happen; unavoidable

A confrontation between the disagreeing neighbors seemed **inevitable**.

A344

adj.—a situation calling for immediate attention; needing more than is reasonable

The **exigent** request for more assistance was answered quickly.

A345

adj.—being separate from others or being reserved

Rolonda's friends have become more **distant** in recent years.

Questions

Q346

DEFERENCE

*Your Own Answer*_____

Q347

DOCUMENT

*Your Own Answer*_____

Q348

DICHOTOMY

*Your Own Answer*_____

Correct Answers

A346

n.—a yielding of opinion; courteous respect for

To avoid a confrontation, the man showed **deference** to his friend.

A347

n.; v.—1. official paper containing information 2. to support; to substantiate; to verify

1. They needed a written **document** to prove that the transaction occurred.

2. Facing an audit, she had to **document** all her client contacts.

A348

n.—a division into two parts or kinds

The **dichotomy** within the party threatens to split it.

Questions

Q349

MINATORY

*Your Own Answer*_____

Q350

ANTAGONISM

*Your Own Answer*_____

Q351

DIATRIBE

*Your Own Answer*_____

Correct Answers

A349

adj.—threatening
The **minatory** stance of the dog warned the thief of an attack.

A350

n.—hostility; opposition
The **antagonism** was created by a misunderstanding.

A351

n.—a bitter or abusive speech
During the divorce hearings, she delivered a **diatribe** full of emotion, pushing her away from her husband.

Questions

DICTUM

*Your Own Answer*_____

EQUIVOCAL

*Your Own Answer*_____

FORAY

*Your Own Answer*_____

Correct Answers

A352

n.—a formal statement of either fact or opinion

Computer programmers have a **dictum**: garbage in, garbage out.

A353

adj.—doubtful; uncertain

Scientific evidence was needed before the **equivocal** hypothesis was accepted by the doubting researchers.

A354

v.; n.—1. to raid for spoils; plunder 2. a sudden attack or raid

1. The soldiers were told not to **foray** the town.
2. The **foray** was a productive way to gain much needed food and supplies.

Questions

Q355

INSULARITY

Your Own Answer

Q356

STOIC

Your Own Answer

Q357

INDOMITABLE

Your Own Answer

Correct Answers

n.—having the characteristics of an island

The **insularity** of the country made it a great place to build a resort.

adj.—detached; unruffled; calm; austere indifference to joy, grief, pleasure, or pain

The soldier had been in week after week of fierce battle; nonetheless, he remained **stoic**.

adj.—not easily discouraged or defeated

The underdog candidate had an **indomitable** spirit.

Questions

DENIGRATE

*Your Own Answer*_____

BLITHE

*Your Own Answer*_____

TERSE

*Your Own Answer*_____

Correct Answers

A358

v.—to defame; to blacken or sully; to belittle

After finding out her evil secret, he announced it to the council and **denigrated** her in public.

A359

adj.—happy; cheery; merry; a cheerful disposition

The wedding was a **blithe** celebration.

A360

adj.—concise; abrupt

She believed in getting to the point, so she always gave **terse** answers.

Questions

Q361

SUBLIMINAL

*Your Own Answer*_____

Q362

IMPEDE

*Your Own Answer*_____

Q363

GIBBER

*Your Own Answer*_____

Correct Answers

A361

adj.—below the level of consciousness
Critics of advertising say that it's loaded with **subliminal** messages.

A362

v.—to stop the progress of; to obstruct
The rain **impeded** the work on the building.

A363

v.—to rapidly speak unintelligibly
They did not want him to represent their position in front of the committee since he was prone to **gibbering** when speaking in front of an audience.

Questions

Q364

PARTISAN

*Your Own Answer*_____

Q365

MELODIOUS

*Your Own Answer*_____

Q366

APATHY

*Your Own Answer*_____

Correct Answers

A364

n.; adj.—1. supporter; follower 2. biased; one-sided

1. A **partisan** for the incumbent mayor will not support the challenger.
2. The union president is **partisan** toward minimum-wage legislation.

A365

adj.—pleasing to hear

The **melodious** sounds of the band attracted many onlookers.

A366

n.—lack of emotion or interest

He showed **apathy** when his relative was injured.

Questions

Q367

OBFUSCATE

Your Own Answer

Q368

ABSTEMIOUS

Your Own Answer

Q369

KINSHIP

Your Own Answer

Correct Answers

A367

v.—to darken; to confuse; to bewilder

The lunar eclipse will **obfuscate** the light of the sun.

A368

adj.—sparing in use of food or drinks

If we become stranded in the snowstorm, we will have to be **abstemious** with our food supply.

A369

n.—family relationship; affinity

Living in close proximity increased the **kinship** of the family.

Questions

Q370

ZEPHYR

*Your Own Answer*_____

Q371

PLUMB

*Your Own Answer*_____

Q372

ANAPHYLAXIS

*Your Own Answer*_____

Correct Answers

A370

n.—a gentle wind; a breeze

It was a beautiful day, with a **zephyr** blowing in from the sea.

A371

adj.; v.—1. perfectly straight down 2. to solve

1. The two walls met **plumb** at the corner.

2. I was able to **plumb** the riddle in a few seconds.

A372

n.—an allergic reaction

The boy's severe **anaphylaxis** to a series of medications made writing prescriptions for him a tricky proposition.

Questions

Q373

JETTISON

*Your Own Answer*_____

Q374

NOTORIOUS

*Your Own Answer*_____

Q375

PIQUE

*Your Own Answer*_____

Correct Answers

A373

v.—to throw goods overboard to lighten a vehicle; to discard

To raise the balloon above the storm clouds, they had to **jettison** the ballast.

A374

adj.—infamous; renowned; having an unfavorable connotation

Discovering that her new neighbor was **notorious** for thievery, she decided to purchase an alarm system for her home.

A375

n.; v.—1. resentment at being slighted; 2. to provoke

1. Being passed over for the promotion aroused his **pique**.

2. He **piqued** her interest when he said he loved books by Maya Angelou.

Questions

Q376

DIMINUTIVE

*Your Own Answer*_____

_____

Q377

MATERIALISM

*Your Own Answer*_____

_____

Q378

TEPID

*Your Own Answer*_____

_____

Correct Answers

A376

adj.; n.—1. smaller than average 2. a small person; a word, expressing smallness, formed when a suffix is added

1. They lived in a **diminutive** house.

2. The **diminutive** woman could not see over the counter.

A377

n.—the belief that everything in the universe is explained in terms of matter; the belief that worldly possessions are the be-all and end-all in life

Spiritualists will tell you that **materialism** is only half the story.

A378

adj.—lacking warmth, interest, enthusiasm; lukewarm

The **tepid** bath water was perfect for relaxing after a long day.

Questions

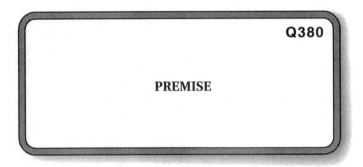

Q379

ACCRUE

*Your Own Answer*_____

Q380

PREMISE

*Your Own Answer*_____

Q381

PANEGYRIC

*Your Own Answer*_____

Correct Answers

v.—to come as natural growth; to increase periodically

Over the course of her college career, she managed to **accrue** a great deal of knowledge.

n.—the basis for an argument

The prosecutor claimed that the defense lawyer's **premise** was shaky, and thus his whole argument was suspect.

n.—high praise

Upon his retirement, he received a great **panegyric** from many of his associates.

Questions

TREPIDATION

*Your Own Answer*_____

AUTHORITARIAN

*Your Own Answer*_____

LEWD

*Your Own Answer*_____

Correct Answers

A382

n.—apprehension; uneasiness

Her long absence caused more than a little **trepidation**.

A383

n.; adj.—1. acting as a dictator 2. demanding obedience

1. The **authoritarian** made all of the rules but did none of the work.

2. Fidel Castro is reluctant to give up his **authoritarian** rule.

A384

adj.—lustful; wicked

The comment was so **lewd** it could not be repeated in front of children.

Questions

PARSIMONIOUS

*Your Own Answer*_____

Q386

DISCORD

*Your Own Answer*_____

Q387

CHIMERA

*Your Own Answer*_____

Correct Answers

A385

adj.—very frugal; unwilling to spend

The owner was so **parsimonious** he refused to purchase new curtains when the old ones fell off the window.

A386

n.—disagreement; lack of harmony

There was **discord** amidst the jury, and therefore a decision could not be made.

A387

n.—an impossible fancy

Perhaps he saw a flying saucer, but perhaps it was only a **chimera**.

Questions

BUCOLIC

*Your Own Answer*_____

ARTICULATE

*Your Own Answer*_____

PREPONDERATE

*Your Own Answer*_____

Correct Answers

A388

adj.—having to do with shepherds or the country

The **bucolic** setting inspired the artist.

A389

v.; adj.—1. to utter clearly and distinctly
2. clear, distinct; expressed with clarity; skillful with words

1. It's even more important to **articulate** your words when you're on the phone.

2. The audience was impressed by the politician's **articulate** speech.

A390

v.—to outweigh; to be superior in amount, weight, etc.

His positive qualities **preponderate** his occasional rudeness.

Questions

Q391

SPELUNKER

*Your Own Answer*_____

Q392

RECUMBENT

*Your Own Answer*_____

Q393

ILLUSORY

*Your Own Answer*_____

Correct Answers

n.—one who studies caves

The **spelunker** made a startling discovery in the old mine.

adj.—resting

The **recumbent** puppy stirred.

adj.—unreal; false; deceptive

He was proven guilty when his alibi was found to be **illusory**.

Questions

Q394

COY

*Your Own Answer*_____

Q395

MANIFEST

*Your Own Answer*_____

Q396

BREVITY

*Your Own Answer*_____

Correct Answers

A394

adj.—modest; bashful; pretending shyness to attract

Her **coy** manners attracted the man.

A395

v.; adj.—1. to show clearly; to appear
2. obvious, clear

1. The image should **manifest** itself as the building when the fog lifts.

2. The **manifest** objective of the war was to push the enemy out of our country.

A396

n.—briefness; shortness

His accident made him ponder the **brevity** of life.

Questions

Q397

GAMUT

*Your Own Answer*_____

Q398

ABOMINATE

*Your Own Answer*_____

Q399

DISPARAGE

*Your Own Answer*_____

Correct Answers

A397

n.—a complete range; any complete musical scale

The woman's wardrobe runs the **gamut** from jeans to suits.

A398

v.—to loathe; to hate

Randall **abominated** all the traffic he encountered on every morning commute.

A399

v.—to belittle; to undervalue; to discredit

After she fired him she realized that she had **disparaged** the value of his assistance.

Questions

Q400

NEOPHYTE

Your Own Answer

Q401

DUBIOUS

Your Own Answer

Q402

RELINQUISH

Your Own Answer

Correct Answers

A400

n.—beginner; newcomer

Critics applauded the **neophyte's** success and speculated how much better he would get with age and experience.

A401

adj.—doubtful; uncertain; skeptical; suspicious

Many people are **dubious** about the possibility of intelligent life on other planets.

A402

v.—to let go; to abandon

House Speaker Jim Wright had to **relinquish** his position after an ethics investigation undermined his authority.

Questions

Q403

EXTANT

*Your Own Answer*_____

Q404

CONTRAVENE

*Your Own Answer*_____

Q405

IMPETUOUS

*Your Own Answer*_____

Correct Answers

adj.—existing; refers especially to books or documents

Some of my ancestor's letters remain **extant**.

v.—to act contrary to; to oppose or contradict

The story of the accused **contravened** the story of the witness.

adj.—moving with great force; done with little thought

The **impetuous** movement took the art community by storm.

Questions

Q406

CATHARSIS

*Your Own Answer*_____

Q407

AUSPICIOUS

*Your Own Answer*_____

Q408

TREK

*Your Own Answer*_____

Correct Answers

A406

n.—a purging or relieving of the body or soul

He experienced a total **catharsis** after the priest absolved his sins.

A407

adj.—being of a good omen; successful

It was **auspicious** that the sun shone on the first day of the trip.

A408

v.—to make a journey

They had to **trek** through the dense forest to reach the nearest village.

Questions

Q409

HERETIC

*Your Own Answer*_____

Q410

FROWARD

*Your Own Answer*_____

Q411

HAMPER

*Your Own Answer*_____

Correct Answers

A409

n.—one who holds an opinion contrary to that which is generally accepted

Because he believed the world was round, many people considered Columbus to be a **heretic**.

A410

adj.—not willing to yield or comply with what is reasonable

The executive had to deal with a **froward** peer who was becoming increasingly difficult.

A411

v.—to interfere with; to hinder

The roadblock **hampered** their progress, but they knew a shortcut.

Questions

Q412

IMPLEMENT

*Your Own Answer*_____

Q413

DOUGHTY

*Your Own Answer*_____

Q414

DISSENT

*Your Own Answer*_____

Correct Answers

A412

v.; n.—1. to carry into effect 2. something used in a given activity

1. In case of emergency **implement** the evacuation plan immediately.

2. The rack is an **implement** of torture.

A413

adj.—brave and strong

The **doughty** fireman saved the woman's life.

A414

v.—to disagree; to differ in opinion

They agreed that something had to be done, but **dissented** on how to do it.

Questions

ABRUPT

*Your Own Answer*_____

VENUE

*Your Own Answer*_____

OBJECTIVE

*Your Own Answer*_____

Correct Answers

A415

adj.—happening or ending unexpectedly

The **abrupt** end to their marriage was a shock to everyone.

A416

n.—location

They had always had their holiday party in the town hall; after 10 years they were ready for a change of **venue**.

A417

adj.; n.—1. open-minded; impartial 2. goal

1. It's hard to set aside your biases and be **objective**.

2. The law student decided that her primary **objective** after graduation was to pass the bar examination.

Questions

Q418

HEDONISTIC

*Your Own Answer*_____

Q419

IMPLACABLE

*Your Own Answer*_____

Q420

DECRY

*Your Own Answer*_____

Correct Answers

A418

adj.—living for pleasure

The group was known for its **hedonistic** rituals and their quest to live life to the fullest.

A419

adj.—unwilling to be pacified or appeased

The baby was so **implacable** a warm bottle would not settle her.

A420

v.—to denounce or condemn openly

The pastor **decried** all forms of discrimination against any minority group.

Questions

TANTALIZE

*Your Own Answer*_____

LIBERTINE

*Your Own Answer*_____

TRUCULENT

*Your Own Answer*_____

Correct Answers

A421

v.—to tempt; to torment

The desserts were **tantalizing**, but he was on a diet.

A422

n.—one who indulges his desires without restraint

For the **libertine**, missing his child's birthday was not as significant as missing a football game.

A423

adj.—fierce; savage; cruel

Truculent fighting broke out in the war-torn country.

Questions

ABDICATE

*Your Own Answer*_____

OPAQUE

*Your Own Answer*_____

SOPORIFIC

*Your Own Answer*_____

Correct Answers

A424

v.—to reject, renounce, or abandon

Due to his poor payment record, it may be necessary to **abdicate** our relationship with the client.

A425

adj.—dull; cloudy; nontransparent

Not having been washed for years, the once beautiful windows of the Victorian home became **opaque**.

A426

adj.—causing sleep

The **soporific** medication should not be taken when you need to drive.

Questions

CHICANERY

*Your Own Answer*_____

RANT

*Your Own Answer*_____

DESPOTISM

*Your Own Answer*_____

Correct Answers

A427

n.—trickery or deception

The swindler was trained in **chicanery**.

A428

v.—to speak in a loud, pompous manner; to rave

He disputed the bill with the shipper, **ranting** that he was dealing with thieves.

A429

n.—tyranny; absolute power or influence

The ruler's **despotism** went uncontested for 30 years.

Questions

ECCLESIASTIC

*Your Own Answer*_____

VAGARY

*Your Own Answer*_____

SUBTLETY

*Your Own Answer*_____

Correct Answers

adj.—pertaining or relating to a church
Ecclesiastic obligations include attending mass.

n.—an odd or eccentric action
His talking to trees was a **vagary** to his puzzled neighbors.

n.—propensity of understatement; so slight as to be barely noticeable
There was no **subtlety** in the protest; each person carried a sign and yelled for civil rights.

Questions

Q433

FUNDAMENTAL

*Your Own Answer*_____

Q434

SERRATED

*Your Own Answer*_____

Q435

SODDEN

*Your Own Answer*_____

Correct Answers

A433

adj.—basic; necessary

Shelter is one of the **fundamental** needs of human existence.

A434

adj.—having a saw-toothed edge

While camping, the family used a **serrated** handsaw to cut firewood.

A435

adj.—soggy; dull in action as if from alcohol

The flowers were **sodden** after the rain.

Questions

REPUGNANT

*Your Own Answer*_____

NETTLE

*Your Own Answer*_____

RECESSION

*Your Own Answer*_____

Correct Answers

A436

adj.—contradictory; distasteful; resistant; offensive

The **repugnant** actions of the man made others lose trust in him.

A437

n.; v.—1. a plant used for spinning fiber
2. to annoy; to irritate
1. The man picked the **nettle** out of the loom to help it work better.
2. The younger brother **nettled** his older sister until she slapped him.

A438

n.—withdrawal; economic downturn

The closing of the factory caused a **recession** in the small town.

Questions

Q439

IMPLICATION

*Your Own Answer*_____

Q440

ASSESS

*Your Own Answer*_____

Q441

PROPINQUITY

*Your Own Answer*_____

Correct Answers

A439

n.—suggestion; inference

An **implication** was made that there might be trickery involved.

A440

v.—to estimate the value of

She **assessed** the possible rewards to see if the project was worth her time and effort.

A441

n.—closeness in time or place; closeness of relationship

The **propinquity** of the disasters put the community in chaos.

Questions

NOVEL

*Your Own Answer*_____

CONSORT

*Your Own Answer*_____

THRALL

*Your Own Answer*_____

Correct Answers

A442

n.; adj.—1. a fictional book; a long story 2. new

1. The **novel** took place in ancient Egypt.
2. It was a **novel** idea for the rock group to play classical music.

A443

n.; v.—1. a companion, spouse 2. to associate

1. An elderly woman was seeking a **consort**.

2. They waited until dark to **consort** under the moonlight.

A444

n.—a slave

The worker was treated like a **thrall**, having to work many hours of overtime.

Questions

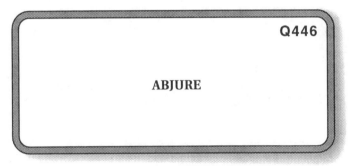

Q445

NEBULOUS

*Your Own Answer*_____

Q446

ABJURE

*Your Own Answer*_____

Q447

PARITY

*Your Own Answer*_____

Correct Answers

A445

adj.—unclear or vague

The ten-page directions were a collection of **nebulous** words and figures.

A446

v.—to give up

The losing team may **abjure** to the team that is winning.

A447

n.—state of being the same in power, value, or rank

When the younger brother was promoted to co-president with the elder son, it established **parity** between the two.

Questions

Q448

SUPERFLUOUS

*Your Own Answer*_____

Q449

TORTUOUS

*Your Own Answer*_____

Q450

AMELIORATE

*Your Own Answer*_____

Correct Answers

adj.—unnecessary; extra

Although the designer considered the piece **superfluous**, the woman wanted the extra chair in her bedroom.

adj.—full of twists and turns; not straightforward; possibly deceitful

The suspect confessed after becoming confused by the **tortuous** questioning of the captain.

v.—to improve or make better

A consistent routine of exercise has been shown to **ameliorate** health.

Questions

Q451

JEOPARDY

*Your Own Answer*_____

Q452

DIFFIDENCE

*Your Own Answer*_____

Q453

ATYPICAL

*Your Own Answer*_____

Correct Answers

A451

n.—danger; peril

The campers realized they were in potential **jeopardy** when the bears surrounded their camp.

A452

n.—a hesitation in asserting oneself

A shy person may have great **diffidence** when faced with a problem.

A453

adj.—something that is abnormal

The **atypical** behavior of the wild animal alarmed the hunters.

Questions

Q454

SKULK

*Your Own Answer*_____

Q455

VISIONARY

*Your Own Answer*_____

Q456

PITTANCE

*Your Own Answer*_____

Correct Answers

A454

v.—to move secretly (implies sinister)

The thief **skulked** around the neighborhood hoping to find his next target.

A455

adj.—seen only in the mind; not realistic; impractical

His **visionary** ideas would never be realized.

A456

n.—a small amount

The reward money was only a **pittance** compared to the money lost.

Questions

Q457

INAUDIBLE

*Your Own Answer*_____

Q458

POTABLE

*Your Own Answer*_____

Q459

MODULATE

*Your Own Answer*_____

Correct Answers

A457

adj.—not able to be heard

The signals were **inaudible** when the fans began to cheer.

A458

adj.—drinkable

The liquid was not **potable**, but rather poisonous.

A459

v.—to regulate or adjust; to vary the pitch

He **modulated** the color knob on the television set until the picture was perfect.

Questions

Q460

CONTRITE

*Your Own Answer*_____

Q461

EXHAUSTIVE

*Your Own Answer*_____

Q462

OPTIMIST

*Your Own Answer*_____

Correct Answers

adj.—regretful; sorrowful; having repentance

Regretting his decision not to attend college, the **contrite** man did not lead a very happy life.

adj.—thorough; complete

It took an **exhaustive** effort, using many construction workers, to complete the new home by the deadline.

n.—person who hopes for the best, sees the good side

He's ever the **optimist**, always seeing the glass as half full.

Questions

Q463

PRECEPT

*Your Own Answer*_____

Q464

ARTIFICE

*Your Own Answer*_____

Q465

POLEMICIST

*Your Own Answer*_____

Correct Answers

A463

n.—a rule or direction of moral conduct

The organization believed its members should abide by certain **precepts**.

A464

n.—skill in a craft

The **artifice** of glassmaking takes many years of practice.

A465

n.—a person skilled in argument

The **polemicist** could debate any case skillfully.

Questions

AMITY

*Your Own Answer*_____

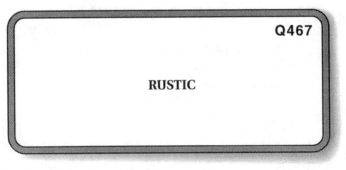

RUSTIC

*Your Own Answer*_____

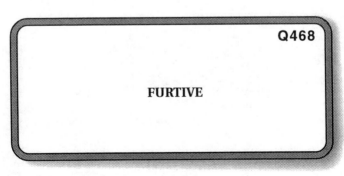

FURTIVE

*Your Own Answer*_____

Correct Answers

A466

n.—friendly relations

The **amity** between the two bordering nations put the populations at ease.

A467

adj.—plain and unsophisticated; homely; of or living in the country

The couple enjoyed spending weekends at their cabin, a **rustic** retreat in the mountains.

A468

adj.—secretive; sly

The detective had much difficulty finding the **furtive** criminal.

Questions

Q469

INNATE

*Your Own Answer*_____

Q470

ENAMORED

*Your Own Answer*_____

Q471

RESONANT

*Your Own Answer*_____

Correct Answers

A469

adj.—natural; inborn

Her talent is wondrous; it hardly matters whether it's **innate** or acquired.

A470

adj.—filled with love and desire

The young couple are **enamored** with each other.

A471

adj.—resounding; reechoing

Beautiful **resonant** music escaped from the cathedral's windows.

Questions

Q472

PERQUISITE

*Your Own Answer*_____

Q473

CONCILIATION

*Your Own Answer*_____

Q474

SUBSTANTIVE

*Your Own Answer*_____

Correct Answers

A472

n.—extra payment; a tip

The waiter was surprised by the extravagant **perquisite** left by the diners.

A473

n.—an attempt to bring together, soothe, or win over

The **conciliation** was successful in that the brothers were speaking again.

A474

adj.—existing independently of others; a large quantity

The only company not acquired in the merger retained its **substantive** existence.

Questions

RESPLENDENT

*Your Own Answer*_____

PRIVY

*Your Own Answer*_____

DETACHED

*Your Own Answer*_____

Correct Answers

A475

adj.—dazzling and shining

Her new diamond was **resplendent** in the sunshine.

A476

adj.—private; confidential

He was one of a handful of people **privy** to the news of the pending merger.

A477

adj.—separated; not interested; standing alone

Detached from modern conveniences, the islanders live a simple, unhurried life.

Questions

PRECLUDE

*Your Own Answer*_____

STOLID

*Your Own Answer*_____

SCHISM

*Your Own Answer*_____

Correct Answers

A478

v.—to inhibit; to make impossible

A healthy diet and lifestyle will not **preclude** your getting ill, although it improves your immune system.

A479

adj.—showing little emotion

With a **stolid** expression, the man walked away from the confrontation.

A480

n.—a division in an organized group

When the group could not decide on a plan of action, a **schism** occurred.

Questions

Q481

FINITE

*Your Own Answer*_____

Q482

EUPHEMISM

*Your Own Answer*_____

Q483

CODIFY

*Your Own Answer*_____

Correct Answers

A481

adj.—measurable; limited; not everlasting

It was discovered decades ago that the universe is not **finite**; it has unknown limits that cannot be measured.

A482

n.—the use of a word or phrase in place of one that is distasteful

The announcer used a **euphemism** when he wanted to complain.

A483

v.—to organize laws or rules into a systematic collection

The laws were **codified** by those whom they affected.

Questions

CORRELATE

*Your Own Answer*_____

COGNATE

*Your Own Answer*_____

ADVERSARY

*Your Own Answer*_____

Correct Answers

v.—to bring into mutual relation

The service man was asked to **correlate** the two computer demonstration pamphlets.

adj.; n.—1. having the same family 2. a person related through ancestry

1. English and German are **cognate** languages.

2. The woman was a **cognate** to the royal family.

n.—an enemy; foe

The peace treaty united two countries that were historically great **adversaries**.

Questions

Q487

MENTOR

*Your Own Answer*_____

Q488

ROSEATE

*Your Own Answer*_____

Q489

ANOMALY

*Your Own Answer*_____

Correct Answers

A487

n.—a teacher; a wise and faithful advisor

Alan consulted his **mentor** when he needed critical advice.

A488

adj.—rose-colored

The **roseate** sunset faded into the sky.

A489

n.—an oddity, inconsistency; a deviation from the norm

An **anomaly** existed when the report listed one statistic, and the spokeswoman reported another.

Questions

Q490

INELUCTABLE

*Your Own Answer*_____

Q491

PRESAGE

*Your Own Answer*_____

Q492

OBJURGATE

*Your Own Answer*_____

Correct Answers

A490

adj.—something inevitable
They were prepared for the **ineluctable** disaster.

A491

n.—an omen; a foreshadowing characteristic
They considered the rainbow at their wedding a
presage for a happy life.

A492

v.—to chide vehemently
The girls disliked those boys who **objurgated**
the group.

Questions

Q493

RISIBLE

*Your Own Answer*_____

Q494

GLIB

*Your Own Answer*_____

Q495

VERITY

*Your Own Answer*_____

Correct Answers

A493

adj.—amusing

The **risible** speech made the audience chuckle.

A494

adj.—smooth and slippery; speaking or spoken in a smooth manner

The salesman was so **glib** that the customers failed to notice the defects in the stereo.

A495

n.—truthfulness

His testimony was given with strict **verity**.

Questions

Q496

FORTITUDE

*Your Own Answer*_____

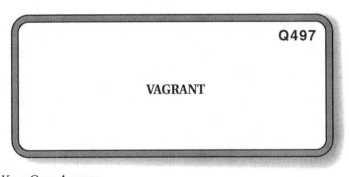

Q497

VAGRANT

*Your Own Answer*_____

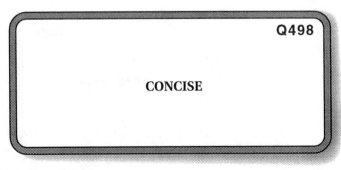

Q498

CONCISE

*Your Own Answer*_____

Correct Answers

A496

n.—firm courage; strength

It is necessary to have **fortitude** to complete the hike.

A497

n.; adj.—1. homeless person 2. rambling; wandering; transient

1. The first thing the shop owner did every morning was chase a **vagrant** from her doorstep.

2. Circus performers, with nary an opportunity to put down roots, typically lead a **vagrant** life.

A498

adj.—in few words; brief; condensed

The **concise** instructions were printed on two pages rather than the customary five.

Questions

Q499

ANACHRONISM

*Your Own Answer*_____

Q500

VINDICATE

*Your Own Answer*_____

Q501

UNCOUTH

*Your Own Answer*_____

Correct Answers

A499

n.—something out of place in time (e.g., an airplane in 1492)

The editor recognized an **anachronism** in the manuscript where the character from the 1500s boarded an airplane.

A500

v.—to clear or defend against criticism or blame

He hired a lawyer to help **vindicate** him in court.

A501

adj.—uncultured; crude

The social club would not accept an **uncouth** individual.

Questions

ENIGMATIC

*Your Own Answer*_____

PRODIGAL

*Your Own Answer*_____

NOSTRUM

*Your Own Answer*_____

Correct Answers

A502

adj.—baffling

The **enigmatic** murder plagued the detective.

A503

adj.—wasteful; lavish

The actor's **prodigal** lifestyle ultimately led to his undoing.

A504

n.—a questionable remedy for difficulties

The doctor's prescription was so unusual that it could be seen as a **nostrum**.

Questions

Q505

TRANSPIRE

*Your Own Answer*_____

Q506

ASPERITY

*Your Own Answer*_____

Q507

TUMULT

*Your Own Answer*_____

Correct Answers

A505

v.—to take place; to come about

With all that's **transpired** today, I'm exhausted.

A506

n.—harshness

The man used **asperity** to frighten the girl out of going.

A507

n.—a noisy commotion; disturbance

The **tumult** was caused by two boys wanting the same toy.

Questions

Q508

INCOMPATIBLE

*Your Own Answer*_____

Q509

INDEMNIFY

*Your Own Answer*_____

Q510

ESCHEW

*Your Own Answer*_____

Correct Answers

A508

adj.—disagreeing; disharmonious; not compatible

The couple decided to end their relationship after realizing they were **incompatible**.

A509

v.—to insure against or pay for loss or damage

It is important to **indemnify** your valuables with a reliable insurance company.

A510

v.—to shun; to avoid

Despite his strong denials, it turned out that the mayoral candidate had not **eschewed** gifts from a big polluter.

Questions

Q511

PAVILION

*Your Own Answer*_____

Q512

DEARTH

*Your Own Answer*_____

Q513

PERPETUAL

*Your Own Answer*_____

Correct Answers

A511

n.—a large tent or covered area, usually used for entertainment

The wedding **pavilion** was not only beautifully decorated, but also served as welcome protection from a sudden downpour.

A512

n.—scarcity; shortage

A series of coincidental resignations left the firm with a **dearth** of talent.

A513

adj.—never ceasing; continuous

Perpetual pain keeps the woman from walking.

Questions

COMMUNAL

*Your Own Answer*_____

COGNIZANT

*Your Own Answer*_____

MOLTEN

*Your Own Answer*_____

Correct Answers

A514

adj.—shared or common ownership

The **communal** nature of the project made everyone pitch in to help.

A515

adj.—aware of; perceptive

She became alarmed when she was **cognizant** of the man following her.

A516

adj.—melted

Steel becomes **molten** after it is heated to thousands of degrees.

Questions

Q517

ACQUIESCE

*Your Own Answer*_____

Q518

OPALESCENT

*Your Own Answer*_____

Q519

DIVERGE

*Your Own Answer*_____

Correct Answers

A517

v.—to agree without protest

The group **acquiesced** to the new regulations even though they were opposed to them.

A518

adj.—iridescent

Her new nail polish was **opalescent**, making her fingertips look like pearls.

A519

v.—to separate; to split

The path **diverges** at the old barn, one fork leading to the house, and the other leading to the pond.

Questions

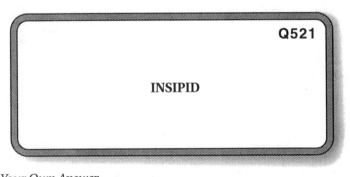

Q520

LETHAL

*Your Own Answer*_____

Q521

INSIPID

*Your Own Answer*_____

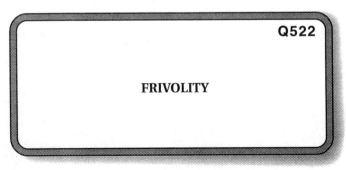

Q522

FRIVOLITY

*Your Own Answer*_____

Correct Answers

A520

adj.—deadly

The natural gas leak caused a **lethal** explosion that killed thousands of innocent people.

A521

adj.—uninteresting; boring; flat; dull

Many people left the **insipid** movie before it was finished.

A522

adj.—giddiness; lack of seriousness

The hardworking students deserved weekend gatherings filled with **frivolity**.

Questions

Q523

ICONOCLAST

*Your Own Answer*_____

Q524

BILATERAL

*Your Own Answer*_____

Q525

ENDEMIC

*Your Own Answer*_____

Correct Answers

A523

n.—one who smashes revered images; an attacker of cherished beliefs

Nietzche's attacks on government, religion, and custom made him an **iconoclast** of grand dimension.

A524

adj.—pertaining to or affecting both sides or two sides; having two sides

A **bilateral** decision was made so that both partners reaped equal benefits from the same amount of work.

A525

adj.—native to a particular area; constantly present in a particular country or locality

The **endemic** fauna was of great interest to the anthropologist.

Questions

Q526

LUNGE

*Your Own Answer*_____

Q527

IMMACULATE

*Your Own Answer*_____

Q528

TRUNCATE

*Your Own Answer*_____

Correct Answers

A526

v.—to move suddenly

The owl will **lunge** at its prey in order to take it off guard.

A527

adj.—perfectly clean; correct; pure

An **immaculate** house is free of dust or clutter.

A528

v.—to shorten by cutting

With the football game running over, the show scheduled to follow it had to be **truncated**.

Questions

Q529

SOLUBILITY

*Your Own Answer*_____

Q530

RAMPART

*Your Own Answer*_____

Q531

REPUDIATE

*Your Own Answer*_____

Correct Answers

A529

n.—that can be solved; that can be dissolved

The **solubility** of sugar causes it to disappear when put in water.

A530

n.;v.—an embankment of earth; any defense 2. to protect

1. The **ramparts** were beginning to crumble under the artillery attack.

2. The invading army failed due to the incessant **rampart** of the guards.

A531

v.—to disown; to deny support for; to reject; to cancel

The man will **repudiate** all claims that he was involved in the deal.

Questions

Q532

ERRONEOUS

*Your Own Answer*_____

Q533

AGGRANDIZE

*Your Own Answer*_____

Q534

DIFFIDENT

*Your Own Answer*_____

Correct Answers

A532

adj.—untrue; inaccurate; not correct

The reporter's **erroneous** story was corrected by a new article that stated the truth.

A533

v.—to make more powerful

The king wanted to **aggrandize** himself and his kingdom.

A534

adj.—timid; lacking self-confidence

The director is looking for a self-assured actor, not a **diffident** one.

Questions

Q535

UPSHOT

*Your Own Answer*_____

Q536

COWER

*Your Own Answer*_____

Q537

USURY

*Your Own Answer*_____

Correct Answers

A535

n.—the final act or result

The **upshot** of the debate was that the bill would be released to the floor.

A536

v.—to huddle and tremble

The lost dog **cowered** near the tree.

A537

n.—the lending of money with an excessively high interest rate

An interest rate 30 points above the prime rate would be considered **usury** in the United States.

Questions

Q538

CONJURE

*Your Own Answer*_____

Q539

OBSEQUIOUS

*Your Own Answer*_____

Q540

COLLOQUIAL

*Your Own Answer*_____

Correct Answers

A538

v.—to call upon or appeal to; to cause to be, appear, come

The smell of the dinner **conjured** images of childhood.

A539

adj.—servilely attentive; fawning

His **obsequious** behavior towards the woman made her feel loved and cared for.

A540

adj.—having to do with conversation; informal speech

The **colloquial** reference indicated the free spirit of the group.

Questions

Q541

CODA

*Your Own Answer*_____

Q542

IRREPARABLE

*Your Own Answer*_____

Q543

RESPITE

*Your Own Answer*_____

Correct Answers

A541

n.—in music, a concluding passage

By the end of the **coda**, I was ready to burst with excitement over the thrilling performance.

A542

adj.—that which cannot be repaired or regained

The damage to the house after the flood was **irreparable**.

A543

n.—recess; rest period

The workers talked and drank coffee during the **respite**.

Questions

Q544

BEREFT

*Your Own Answer*_____

Q545

INVETERATE

*Your Own Answer*_____

Q546

GENIAL

*Your Own Answer*_____

Correct Answers

A544

v.—to be deprived of; to be in a sad manner

The loss of his job will leave the man **bereft** of many luxuries.

A545

adj.—a practice settled on over a long period of time

The **inveterate** induction ceremony bespoke one of the school's great traditions.

A546

adj.—contributing to life; amiable

Key West's **genial** climate is among its many attractive aspects.

Questions

Q547

WHET

*Your Own Answer*_____

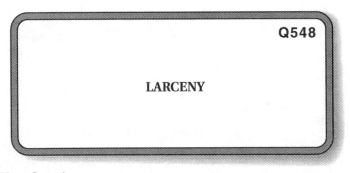

Q548

LARCENY

*Your Own Answer*_____

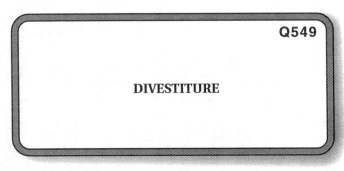

Q549

DIVESTITURE

*Your Own Answer*_____

Correct Answers

A547

v.—to sharpen by rubbing; to stimulate

Before carving the turkey, you must **whet** the blade.

A548

n.—theft; stealing

After robbing the liquor store, she was found guilty of **larceny**.

A549

n.—being stripped

When it was found the team cheated, there was a **divestiture** of their crown.

Questions

Q550

IMPERVIOUS

*Your Own Answer*_____

Q551

SATURATE

*Your Own Answer*_____

Q552

RANCOR

*Your Own Answer*_____

Correct Answers

A550

adj.—impenetrable; not allowing anything to pass through; unaffected

The vest that the policeman wears is **impervious** to bullets.

A551

v.—to soak thoroughly; to drench

She **saturated** the sponge with soapy water before she began washing the car.

A552

n.—strong ill will; enmity

Her **rancor** for the man was evident in her hateful expression.

Questions

Q553

COHESION

Your Own Answer _____

Q554

PLENARY

Your Own Answer _____

Q555

APPOSITE

Your Own Answer _____

Correct Answers

A553

n.—the act of holding together

The **cohesion** of the group increased as friend-ships were formed.

A554

adj.—full; entire; complete

A **plenary** class of students staged the protest.

A555

adj.—suitable; apt; relevant

Discussion of poverty was **apposite** to the curriculum, so the professor allowed it.

Questions

Q556

LITHE

*Your Own Answer*_____

Q557

ALTRUISM

*Your Own Answer*_____

Q558

CONJOIN

*Your Own Answer*_____

Correct Answers

A556

adj.—easily bent; pliable; supple

It is best to use a **lithe** material when constructing a curved object.

A557

n.—unselfish devotion to the welfare of others

The organization was given an award for **altruism** after aiding those left homeless by the flood.

A558

v.—to combine

The classes will **conjoin** to do the play.

Questions

SAVANT

*Your Own Answer*_____

GOAD

*Your Own Answer*_____

INCHOATE

*Your Own Answer*_____

Correct Answers

n.—one who is intelligent
The **savant** accepted his award of excellence.

n.; v.—1. a driving impulse 2. to push into action
1. His **goad** urged him to pursue the object of his affection.
2. Thinking about money will **goad** him into getting a job.

adj.—not yet fully formed; rudimentary
The **inchoate** building appeared as if it would be a fast-food restaurant.

Questions

Q562

DELUSION

*Your Own Answer*_____

Q563

BAROQUE

*Your Own Answer*_____

Q564

PHENOMENON

*Your Own Answer*_____

Correct Answers

A562

n.—a false belief or opinion

The historian suffered from the **delusion** that he was Napoleon.

A563

adj.—extravagant; ornate; embellished

The **baroque** artwork was made up of intricate details that kept the museum-goers enthralled.

A564

n.—an exceptional person; an unusual occurrence

They called Yankee Stadium "The House that Ruth Built" because the Babe was a **phenomenon**.

Questions

Q565

CANARD

*Your Own Answer*_____

Q566

QUIESCENT

*Your Own Answer*_____

Q567

IMPROVIDENT

*Your Own Answer*_____

Correct Answers

A565

n.—a false statement or rumor

The **canard** was reported in a scandalous tabloid.

A566

adj.—inactive; at rest

Everyone deserves a day off and should remain **quiescent** at least one day a week.

A567

adj.—not providing for the future

An **improvident** person may end up destitute in later life.

Questions

Q568

CABAL

*Your Own Answer*_____

Q569

PARODY

*Your Own Answer*_____

Q570

RECONDITE

*Your Own Answer*_____

Correct Answers

A568

n.—a group of persons joined by a secret

The very idea that there could be a **cabal** cast suspicion on the whole operation.

A569

n.—a piece of work imitating another in a satirical manner; a poor imitation

The play was a **parody** of the king and queen's marital difficulties.

A570

adj.—hard to understand; concealed

The students were dumbfounded by the **recondite** topic.

Questions

Q571

GUILE

*Your Own Answer*_____

Q572

CENSOR

*Your Own Answer*_____

Q573

UNIFORM

*Your Own Answer*_____

Correct Answers

A571

n.—slyness; deceit

By using his **guile**, the gambler almost always won at the card table.

A572

v.—to examine and delete objectionable material

The children were allowed to watch the adult movie only after it had been **censored**.

A573

n.; adj.; v.—1. official or distinctive clothes; never changing 2. always with the same standard 3. to clothe or supply with uniforms; to make the same

1. The boy scout's **uniforms** were olive green.
2. The marching band moved in **uniform** across the field.
3. The first task of the general was to **uniform** his men.

Questions

Q574

PLAINTIVE

*Your Own Answer*_____

Q575

AFFILIATE

*Your Own Answer*_____

Q576

TENUOUS

*Your Own Answer*_____

Correct Answers

adj.—being mournful or sad
His wife's death made Sam **plaintive**.

v.; n.—1. to connect or associate with; to accept as a member 2. a member of an organization

1. The hiking club **affiliated** with the bird-watching club.
2. The **affiliate** with the most sway is the founding member.

adj.—thin, slim, delicate; weak
The hurricane force winds ripped the **tenuous** branches from the tree.

Questions

Q577

PUNGENT

*Your Own Answer*_____

Q578

IRREPROACHABLE

*Your Own Answer*_____

Q579

RECIPROCAL

*Your Own Answer*_____

Correct Answers

A577

adj.—sharp; stinging

When the refrigerator door opened, the smell of lemons was **pungent**.

A578

adj.—without blame or faults

The honesty of the priest made him **irreproachable**.

A579

adj.—mutual; having the same relationship to each other

Hernando's membership in the Picture of Health Fitness Center gives him **reciprocal** privileges at 245 health clubs around the United States.

Questions

Q580

PLAUSIBLE

*Your Own Answer*_____

Q581

QUANDARY

*Your Own Answer*_____

Q582

VERTIGO

*Your Own Answer*_____

Correct Answers

A580

adj.—probable; feasible

After weeks of trying to determine what or who was raiding the chicken coop, the farmer came up with a **plausible** explanation.

A581

n.—dilemma

Tristan and Elizabeth were caught in a **quandary**: should they spend Thanksgiving with his parents or hers?

A582

n.—a sensation of dizziness

After her car was hit from behind, the driver experienced **vertigo** when her head hit the steering wheel.

Questions

ACCOMPLICE

*Your Own Answer*_____

COVENANT

*Your Own Answer*_____

DEPOSITION

*Your Own Answer*_____

Correct Answers

A583

n.—co-conspirator; partner; partner-in-crime
The bank robber's **accomplice** drove the get-
away car.

A584

n.—a binding and solemn agreement
With the exchange of vows, the **covenant** was
complete.

A585

n.—a removal from office or power; a testimony
Failing to act lawfully could result in his **deposition**.

Questions

STEADFAST

*Your Own Answer*_____

ADULTERATE

*Your Own Answer*_____

INCONCLUSIVE

*Your Own Answer*_____

Correct Answers

A586

adj.—loyal

The Secret Service agents are **steadfast** to their oath to protect the president.

A587

v.—to corrupt, debase, or make impure

The dumping of chemicals will **adulterate** the pureness of the lake.

A588

adj.—not final or of a definite result

The results being **inconclusive**, the doctors continued to look for a cause of the illness.

Questions

Q589

MALIGN

*Your Own Answer*_____

Q590

UNWONTED

*Your Own Answer*_____

Q591

RENDER

*Your Own Answer*_____

Correct Answers

A589

v.; adj.—1. to speak evil of 2. having an evil disposition toward others (opposite: benign)

1. In her statement to the judge she **maligned** her soon-to-be ex-husband.

2. She had such a **malign** personality that no one even tried to approach her, mostly out of fear.

A590

adj.—rare

The **unwonted** raise would be the only one received for a few years.

A591

v.—to deliver; to provide

The Yorkville First Aid Squad was first on the scene to **render** assistance.

Questions

Q592

INANIMATE

*Your Own Answer*_____

Q593

CAUSTIC

*Your Own Answer*_____

Q594

NOSTALGIC

*Your Own Answer*_____

Correct Answers

A592

adj.—to be dull or spiritless; not animated, not endowed with life

The boy nagged his father for a real puppy, not some **inanimate** stuffed animal.

A593

adj.—eating away at; marked by sarcasm

The **caustic** chemicals are dangerous.

A594

adj.—longing for the past; filled with bitter-sweet memories

She loved her new life, but became **nostalgic** when she met with her old friends.

Questions

DIRGE

*Your Own Answer*_____

VULNERABLE

*Your Own Answer*_____

REMONSTRATE

*Your Own Answer*_____

Correct Answers

n.—a hymn for a funeral; a song or poem expressing lament

The mourners sang a traditional Irish **dirge**.

adj.—open to attack; unprotected

Deer usually stay in the forest because they know they are **vulnerable** in open areas.

v.—to protest or object to

The population will **remonstrate** against the new taxes.

Questions

Q598

KINDLE

*Your Own Answer*_____

Q599

ELABORATION

*Your Own Answer*_____

Q600

DESCANT

*Your Own Answer*_____

Correct Answers

A598

v.—to ignite; to arouse

Being around children **kindled** her interest in educational psychology.

A599

n.—act of clarifying; adding details

The mayor called for an **elaboration** on the ordinance's first draft.

---

n.; v.—1. a varied song or melody; a song **A600** for two people with separate melodies for each singer 2. lengthy talking or writing

1. The **descant** performed by the pair of monks proved to be the highlight of dinner.
2. The man will **descant** on the subject if you give him too much speaking time.

Questions

Q601

ACCRETION

*Your Own Answer*_____

Q602

HEFTY

*Your Own Answer*_____

Q603

CENSURE

*Your Own Answer*_____

Correct Answers

n.—growth by addition; a growing together by parts

With the **accretion** of the new members, the club doubled its original size.

adj.—heavy or powerful

The unabridged dictionary makes for a **hefty** book.

n.; v.—1. a disapproval; an expression of disapproval 2. to criticize or disapprove of

1. His remarks drew the **censure** of his employers.

2. In order to **censure** his work, the editor asked for the story earlier than expected.

Questions

Q604

BESTIAL

*Your Own Answer*_____

Q605

OSTRACIZE

*Your Own Answer*_____

Q606

ARID

*Your Own Answer*_____

Correct Answers

A604

adj.—having the qualities of a beast; brutal

The **bestial** employer made his employees work in an unheated room.

A605

v.—to exclude

The students tend to **ostracize** the children they dislike from their games.

A606

adj.—extremely dry, parched; barren, unimaginative

The terrain was so **arid** that not one species of plant could survive.

Questions

Q607

AUGMENT

*Your Own Answer*_____

Q608

PEDESTRIAN

*Your Own Answer*_____

Q609

BALEFUL

*Your Own Answer*_____

Correct Answers

v.—to increase or add to; to make larger

They needed more soup so they **augmented** the recipe.

adj.; n.—1. mediocre; ordinary 2. a person who walks

1. We expected the meal to be exceptional, but it was just **pedestrian**.
2. The car almost hit the **pedestrian** as she crossed the street.

adj.—harmful, malign, detrimental

After she was fired, she realized it was a **baleful** move to point the blame at her superior.

Questions

ELEGY

*Your Own Answer*_____

COLLUSION

*Your Own Answer*_____

PUERILE

*Your Own Answer*_____

Correct Answers

A610

n.—a poem of lament and praise for the dead
Upon conclusion of the **elegy**, the casket was closed.

A611

n.—secret agreement for an illegal purpose
The authority discovered a **collusion** between the director and treasurer.

A612

adj.—childlike; silly
The **puerile** actions of the man caused him to lose his promotion.

Questions

Q613

HARMONIOUS

*Your Own Answer*_____

Q614

BIENNIAL

*Your Own Answer*_____

Q615

CACOPHONOUS

*Your Own Answer*_____

Correct Answers

A613

adj.—having proportionate and orderly parts

The challenge for the new conductor was to mold his musicians' talents into a **harmonious** orchestra.

A614

adj.; n.—1. happening every two years 2. a plant that blooms every two years

1. The **biennial** journal's influence seemed only magnified by its infrequent publication.

2. She has lived here for four years and has seen the **biennials** bloom twice.

A615

adj.—sounding jarring

The **cacophonous** sound from the bending metal sent shivers up our spines.

Questions

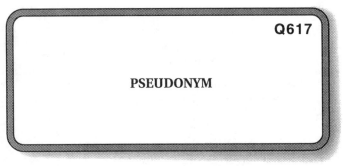

Q616

URBANE

*Your Own Answer*_____

Q617

PSEUDONYM

*Your Own Answer*_____

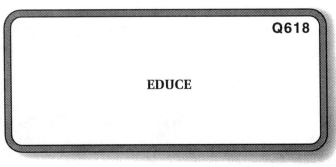

Q618

EDUCE

*Your Own Answer*_____

Correct Answers

adj.—cultured; suave

The gala concert and dinner dance was attended by the most **urbane** individuals.

n.—a borrowed or fictitious name

Larry was a **pseudonym** for the reporter who did not want to use his real name.

v.—to draw out; to infer from information

Because she is so dour, I was forced to **educe** a response.

Questions

Q619

INERT

*Your Own Answer*_____

Q620

POLEMIC

*Your Own Answer*_____

Q621

PALATIAL

*Your Own Answer*_____

Correct Answers

A619

adj.—not reacting chemically; inactive

Inert gases such as krypton and argon can enhance window insulation.

A620

adj.; n.—1. controversial 2. an argument or controversial discussion; a person inclined to argument

1. The **polemic** decision caused a stir in the community.
2. The **polemic** ended his evening with yet another heated discussion on politics.

A621

adj.—large and ornate, like a palace

The new **palatial** home contained two pools and an indoor track for jogging.

Questions

GENERIC

*Your Own Answer*_____

COGENT

*Your Own Answer*_____

CONSECRATE

*Your Own Answer*_____

Correct Answers

A622

adj.—common; general; universal

While **generic** drugs are often a better value, it is always a good idea to consult your doctor before purchasing them.

A623

adj.—to the point; clear; convincing in its clarity and presentation

The lawyer made compelling and **cogent** presentations, which evidently helped him win 96 percent of his cases.

A624

v.—to declare sacred; to dedicate

We will **consecrate** the pact during the ceremony.

Questions

Q625

REBUFF

*Your Own Answer*_____

Q626

ENFRANCHISE

*Your Own Answer*_____

Q627

IRRATIONAL

*Your Own Answer*_____

Correct Answers

A625

n.—a blunt refusal to offered help

The **rebuff** of her aid plan came as a shock.

A626

v.—to free from obligation; to admit to citizenship

The player was **enfranchised** when the deal was called off.

A627

adj.—not logical

It would be **irrational** to climb Mt. Everest without some very warm clothing.

Questions

COMPLIANT

*Your Own Answer*_____

FETISH

*Your Own Answer*_____

MALICIOUS

*Your Own Answer*_____

Correct Answers

adj.—complying; obeying; yielding
Compliant actions should be reinforced.

n.—anything to which one gives excessive devotion
The clay figure of a fertility goddess was a **fetish** from an ancient civilization.

adj.—spiteful; vindictive
The **malicious** employee slashed her manager's tires for revenge.

Questions

Q631

BESMIRCH

*Your Own Answer*_____

Q632

HOMILY

*Your Own Answer*_____

Q633

POMMEL

*Your Own Answer*_____

Correct Answers

A631

v.—to dirty or discolor

The soot from the chimney will **besmirch** clean curtains.

A632

n.—solemn moral talk; sermon

The preacher gave a moving **homily** to the gathered crowd.

A633

n.—the rounded, upward-projecting front of a saddle

The woman was so nervous about being on the horse she would not let go of the **pommel**.

Questions

Q634

CONTUMACIOUS

*Your Own Answer*_____

Q635

DENOUNCE

*Your Own Answer*_____

Q636

PEJORATIVE

*Your Own Answer*_____

Correct Answers

adj.—resisting authority

The man was put in jail for **contumacious** actions.

v.—to speak out against; to condemn

A student rally was called to **denounce** the use of drugs on campus.

adj.—making things worse

The **pejorative** comment deepened the dislike between the two families.

Questions

Q637

METTLE

*Your Own Answer*_____

Q638

INNUENDO

*Your Own Answer*_____

Q639

MYRIAD

*Your Own Answer*_____

Correct Answers

A637

n.—spirit, courage, ardor

He proved he had the **mettle** to make it through basic training.

A638

n.—an indirect remark; an insinuation

The student made an **innuendo** referring to the professor.

A639

n.—a large number

Buying an old house often necessitates fixing a **myriad** of problems.

Questions

Q640

ABJECT

*Your Own Answer*_____

Q641

INSOLVENT

*Your Own Answer*_____

Q642

ENNUI

*Your Own Answer*_____

Correct Answers

A640

adj.—of the worst or lowest degree

The Haldemans lived in **abject** poverty, with barely a roof over their heads.

A641

adj.—unable to pay debts

The **insolvent** state of his bank account kept him from writing any checks.

A642

n.—boredom; apathy

The endless speech by the CEO produced an unbearable **ennui** which led many of the employees to fall asleep.

Questions

DECIDUOUS

Your Own Answer

ABSTRACT

Your Own Answer

ARROGATE

Your Own Answer

Correct Answers

A643

adj.—shedding; temporary

When the leaves began to fall from the tree we learned that it was **deciduous**.

---

adj.; n.; v.—1. not easy to understand; theoretical 2. a brief statement in summary 3. to take away; to remove **A644**

1. Gauss' law can seem very **abstract** unless you're a mathemetician.
2. The report's **abstract** was enough to sway the decision.
3. The chemist attempted to **abstract** water from air.

A645

v.—to claim or demand unduly

The teenager **arrogated** that he should be able to use his parent's car whenever he desired.

Questions

PENURIOUS

*Your Own Answer*_____

RIGOR

*Your Own Answer*_____

UNPRECEDENTED

*Your Own Answer*_____

Correct Answers

A646

adj.—stingy, miserly

The **penurious** man had millions of dollars, but lived in a cottage to save money.

A647

n.—the quality of being unyielding; severity

She criticized the planning board's vote with **rigor**.

A648

adj.—unheard of; exceptional

Weeks of intense heat created **unprecedented** power demands, which the utilities were hard-pressed to meet.

Questions

Q649

NARCISSISTIC

*Your Own Answer*_____

Q650

ABBREVIATE

*Your Own Answer*_____

Q651

OCCULT

*Your Own Answer*_____

Correct Answers

A649

adj.—egotistical; self-centered; self-love, excessive interest in one's appearance, comfort, abilities, etc.

The **narcissistic** actor was difficult to get along with.

A650

v.—to shorten; to compress; to diminish

His vacation to Japan was **abbreviated** when he acquired an illness treatable only in the United States.

A651

adj.—hidden; beyond human understanding; mystical; mysterious

The **occult** meaning of the message was one of dislike for the authorities.

Questions

Q652

TRAUMATIC

*Your Own Answer*_____

Q653

INGENUE

*Your Own Answer*_____

Q654

ANCHORAGE

*Your Own Answer*_____

Correct Answers

adj.—causing a violent injury

It was a **traumatic** accident, leaving the driver with a broken vertebra, a smashed wrist, and a concussion.

n.—an unworldly young woman

As an **ingenue**, Corky had no experience outside of her small town.

n.—something that can be relied on

Knowing the neighbors were right next door was an **anchorage** for the elderly woman.

Questions

Q655

HIERARCHY

*Your Own Answer*_____

Q656

LASSITUDE

*Your Own Answer*_____

Q657

CONDONE

*Your Own Answer*_____

Correct Answers

A655

n.—a system of persons or things arranged according to rank

I was put at the bottom of the **hierarchy**, while Jane was put at the top.

A656

n.—being tired or listless

After working a 24-hour shift, the nurses were in a state of **lassitude.**

A657

v.—to overlook; to forgive

The loving and forgiving mother **condoned** her son's life of crime

Questions

Q658

VAUNTED

*Your Own Answer*_____

Q659

CHURLISHNESS

*Your Own Answer*_____

Q660

TIMBRE

*Your Own Answer*_____

Correct Answers

A658

adj.; v.—1. much praised; 2. to boast of

1. Rommel's **vaunted** Afrika Korps was defeated by Montgomery.

2. When her son was accepted to college, she **vaunted** his success to everyone.

A659

n.—crude or surly behavior; behavior of a peasant

The fraternity's **churlishness** ran afoul of the dean's office.

A660

n.—the quality of sound that distinguishes one sound from another

The **timbre** of guitar music is different from that of piano music.

Questions

Q661

IGNOBLE

*Your Own Answer*_____

Q662

HIATUS

*Your Own Answer*_____

Q663

REMORSE

*Your Own Answer*_____

Correct Answers

A661

adj.—ordinary; dishonorable

The king was adamant about keeping his son from wedding an **ignoble** serf.

A662

n.—interval; break; period of rest

Summer vacation provided a much-needed **hiatus** for the students.

A663

n.—guilt; sorrow

The prosecutor argued that the defendant had shown no **remorse** for his actions.

Questions

CURMUDGEON

*Your Own Answer*_____

NEOLOGISM

*Your Own Answer*_____

OSTENTATIOUS

*Your Own Answer*_____

Correct Answers

A664

n.—an ill-tempered person
The **curmudgeon** asked the children not to play near the house.

A665

n.—giving a new meaning to an old word
Bad is a **neologism** for good.

A666

adj.—being showy
Sure he'd won the lottery, but coming to work in a stretch limo seemed a bit **ostentatious**.

Questions

Q667

EMANATE

*Your Own Answer*_____

Q668

REDUNDANT

*Your Own Answer*_____

Q669

CESSATION

*Your Own Answer*_____

Correct Answers

A667

v.—to emit

Happiness **emanates** from the loving home.

A668

adj.—wordy; repetitive; unnecessary to the meaning

The **redundant** lecture of the professor repeated the lesson in the text.

A669

n.—ceasing; a stopping

The **cessation** of a bad habit is often difficult to sustain.

Questions

FASTIDIOUS

*Your Own Answer*_____

ARROGANT

*Your Own Answer*_____

VELOCITY

*Your Own Answer*_____

Correct Answers

A670

adj.—difficult to please; dainty

The **fastidious** girl would not accept any offers as suitable.

A671

adj.—acting superior to others; conceited

After purchasing his new, expensive sports car, the **arrogant** doctor refused to allow anyone to ride with him to the country club.

A672

n.—speed

The supersonic transport travels at an amazing **velocity**.

Questions

Q673

GAUCHE

*Your Own Answer*_____

Q674

IMPECUNIOUS

*Your Own Answer*_____

Q675

CIRCUMLOCUTORY

*Your Own Answer*_____

Correct Answers

A673

adj.—awkward; lacking social grace

Unfortunately, the girl was too **gauche** to fit into high society.

A674

adj.—poor; having no money

The Great Depression made family after family **impecunious**.

A675

adj.—being too long, as in a description or expression; a roundabout, indirect, or ungainly way of expressing something

It was a **circumlocutory** documentary that could have been cut to half its running time to say twice as much.

Questions

Q676

PUTREFY

*Your Own Answer*_____

Q677

PRUDENT

*Your Own Answer*_____

Q678

ENHANCE

*Your Own Answer*_____

Correct Answers

A676

v.—to decompose; to rot

Food will begin to **putrefy** if exposed to air for too long.

A677

adj.—wise; careful; prepared

Her **prudent** ways saved her money, time, and trouble.

A678

v.—to improve; to compliment; to make more attractive

The new fuel **enhanced** the performance of the rocket's engines.

Questions

Q679

INSULAR

*Your Own Answer*_____

Q680

VALOR

*Your Own Answer*_____

Q681

STIGMATIZE

*Your Own Answer*_____

Correct Answers

adj.—having the characteristics of an island; narrow-minded; provincial

After walking along the entire perimeter and seeing that the spit of land was actually **insular**, we realized it was time to build a boat.

n.—bravery

She received a medal for her **valor** during the war.

v.—to characterize or mark as disgraceful

The gross error will **stigmatize** the worker as careless.

Questions

Q682

PESSIMISM

*Your Own Answer*_____

Q683

QUARANTINE

*Your Own Answer*_____

Q684

PROLIFIC

*Your Own Answer*_____

Correct Answers

A682

n.—seeing only the gloomy side; hopelessness

After endless years of drought, **pessimism** grew in the hearts of even the most dedicated farmer.

A683

n.; v.—1. isolation of a person or persons to prevent the spread of disease 2. to isolate physically, politically, commercially, or socially

1. To be sure they didn't bring any contagions back to Earth, the astronauts were put under **quarantine** when they returned.
2. The judge **quarantined**, or sequestered, the jury.

A684

adj.—fruitful

The merger resulted in a **prolific** business that became an asset to the community.

Questions

Q685

REPLICA

*Your Own Answer*_____

Q686

TURBID

*Your Own Answer*_____

Q687

INDOLENT

*Your Own Answer*_____

Correct Answers

A685

n.—copy; representation; reproduction

The equine sculpture was a **replica** of a Remington.

A686

adj.—thick and dense; cloudy

The **turbid** green waters of the lake prevented them from seeing the bottom.

A687

adj.—lazy; inactive

If we find him goofing off one more time, we won't be able to escape the fact that he's **indolent**.

Questions

Q688

OAF

*Your Own Answer*_____

Q689

INDIGENOUS

*Your Own Answer*_____

Q690

DISCRIMINATE

*Your Own Answer*_____

Correct Answers

A688

n.—a clumsy, dumb person

The waiter has been called an **oaf** ever since he dropped the tray.

A689

adj.—native to a region; inborn or innate

These plants are **indigenous** to all of the western states.

A690

v.—to distinguish; to demonstrate bias

Being a chef, he **discriminated** carefully among ingredients.

Questions

Q691

WANE

*Your Own Answer*_____

Q692

DERISION

*Your Own Answer*_____

Q693

STAMINA

*Your Own Answer*_____

Correct Answers

v.—to gradually become less; to grow dim

After time, interest in the show will **wane** and it will no longer be as popular.

n.—the act of mocking; ridicule, mockery

A day of **derision** from the boss left the employee feeling depressed.

n.—endurance

Anybody who can finish the New York marathon has **stamina**.

Questions

VALANCE

*Your Own Answer*_____

ABAFT

*Your Own Answer*_____

TRIBUNAL

*Your Own Answer*_____

Correct Answers

n.—short drapery hanging over the window frame

They decided to hang a floral **valance** over the kitchen window.

adv.—on or toward the rear of a ship

The passengers moved **abaft** of the ship so as to escape the fire in the front of the ship.

n.—the seat of a judge; a court of justice

The **tribunal** heard the case of the burglary.

Questions

Q697

PAROCHIAL

*Your Own Answer*_____

Q698

ALCHEMY

*Your Own Answer*_____

Q699

NEFARIOUS

*Your Own Answer*_____

Correct Answers

A697

adj.—religious; narrow-minded
Devout Christians, the Chesterfields enrolled
their children in a **parochial** school.

A698

n.—any mysterious change of substance or
nature
The magician used **alchemy** to change the
powder into a liquid.

A699

adj.—morally bad; wicked
The **nefarious** criminal was the scourge of the
local police force.

Questions

DOTING

*Your Own Answer*_____

INDIFFERENT

*Your Own Answer*_____

TUMID

*Your Own Answer*_____

Correct Answers

A700

adj.—excessively fond of

With great joy, the **doting** father held the toddler.

A701

adj.—unconcerned

There he lay, **indifferent** to all the excitement around him.

A702

adj.—swollen; pompous

The **tumid** river washed away the homes built on the shore.

BLANK CARDS
To Make Up
Your Own Questions

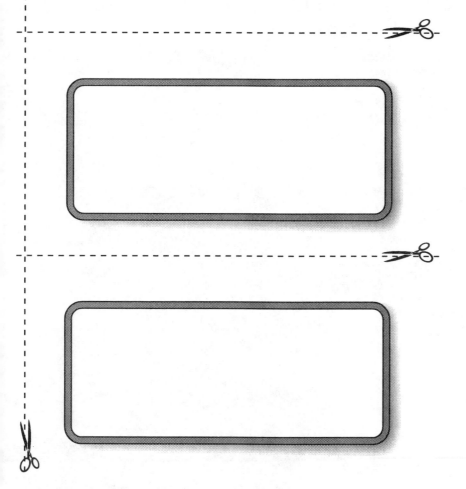

CORRECT ANSWERS

for

Your Own Questions

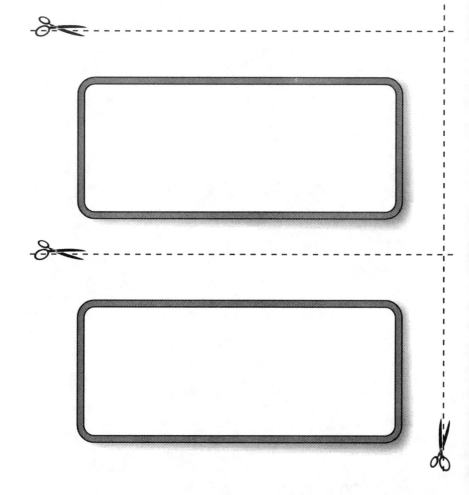

Blank Cards for
Your Own Questions

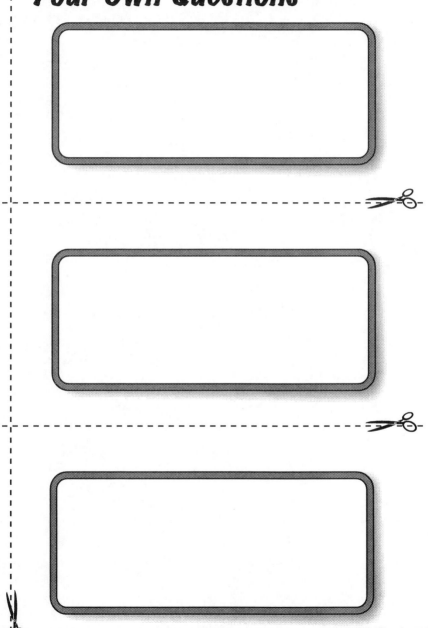

Correct Answers

Blank Cards for *Your Own Questions*

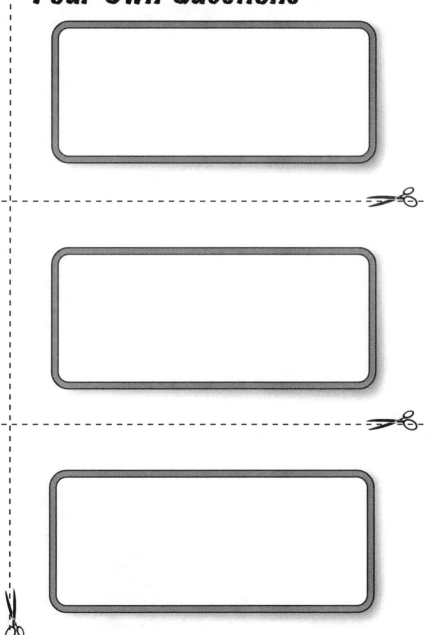

Correct Answers

Blank Cards for
Your Own Questions

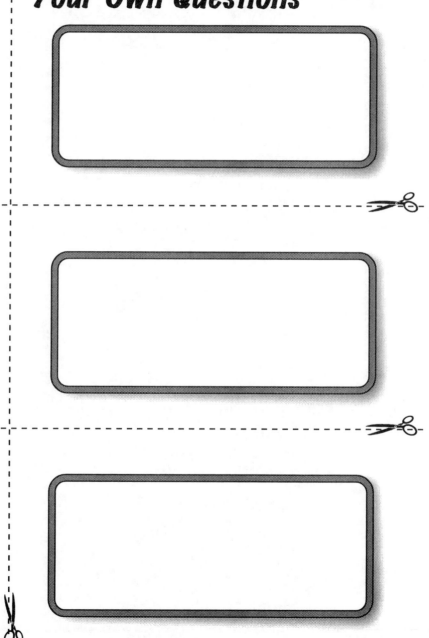

Correct Answers

Blank Cards for
Your Own Questions

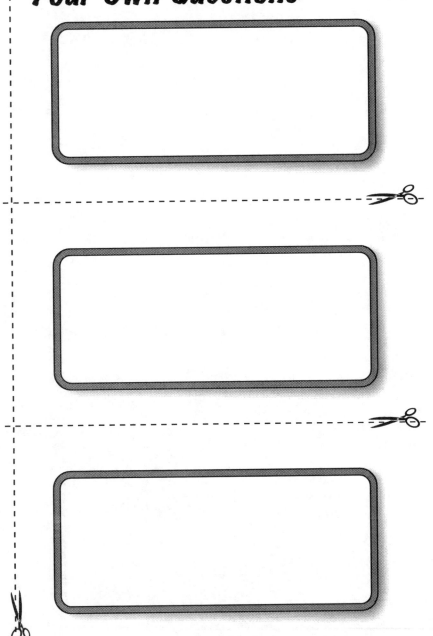

Correct Answers

Blank Cards for
Your Own Questions

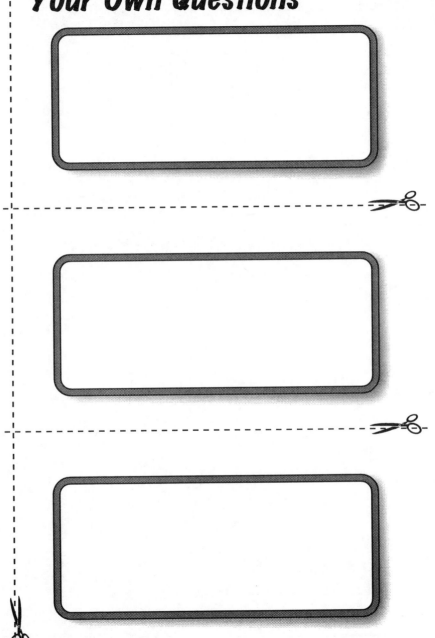

Correct Answers

Blank Cards for *Your Own Questions*

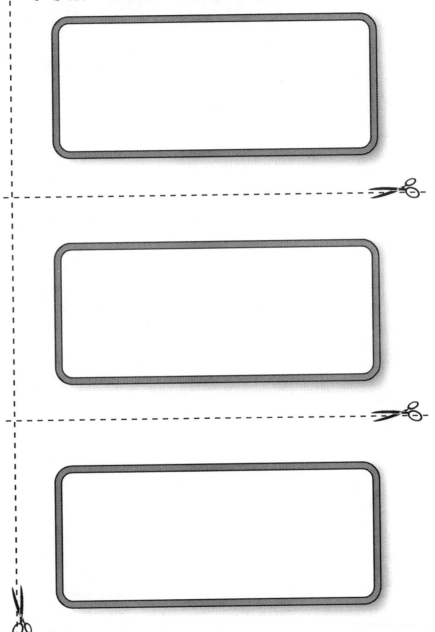

Correct Answers

Blank Cards for
Your Own Questions

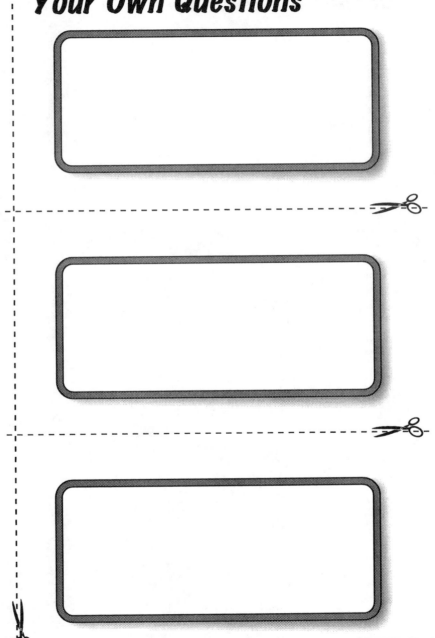

Correct Answers

Blank Cards for *Your Own Questions*

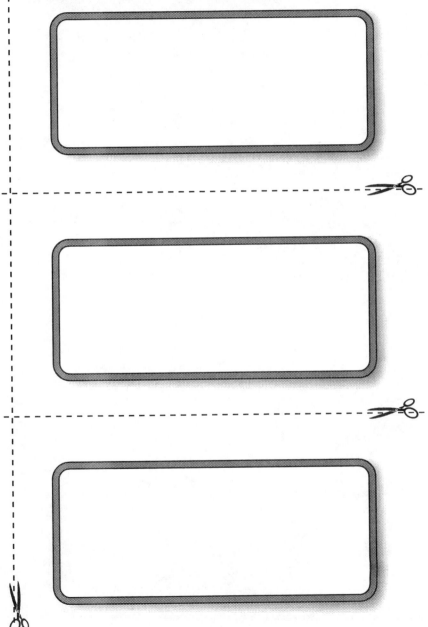

Correct Answers

Blank Cards for *Your Own Questions*

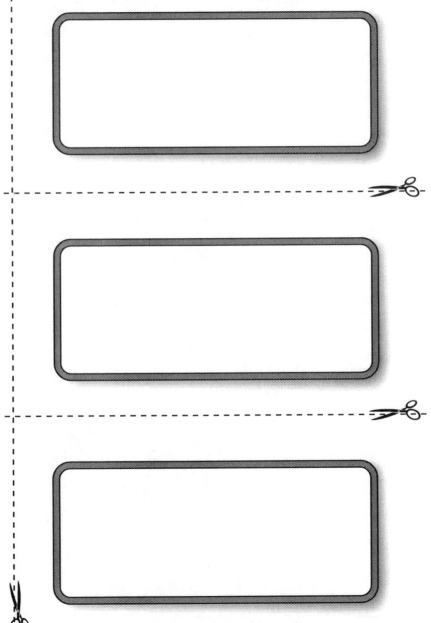

Correct Answers

Blank Cards for *Your Own Questions*

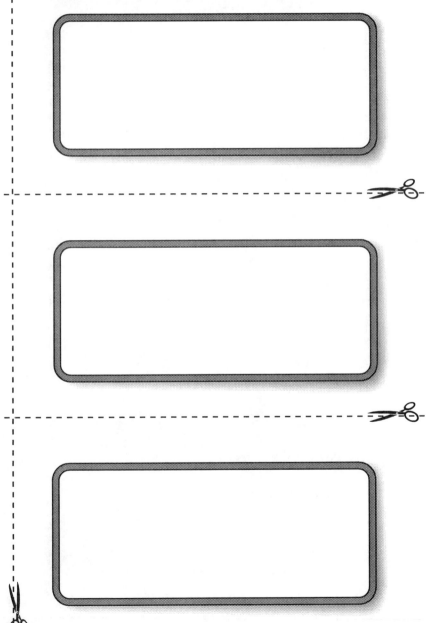

Correct Answers

Blank Cards for *Your Own Questions*

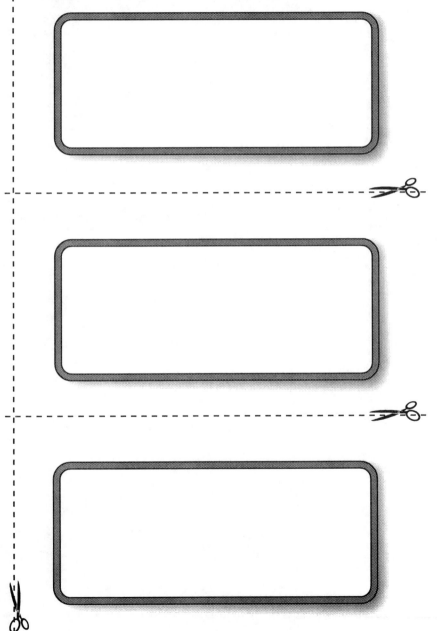

Correct Answers

Blank Cards for *Your Own Questions*

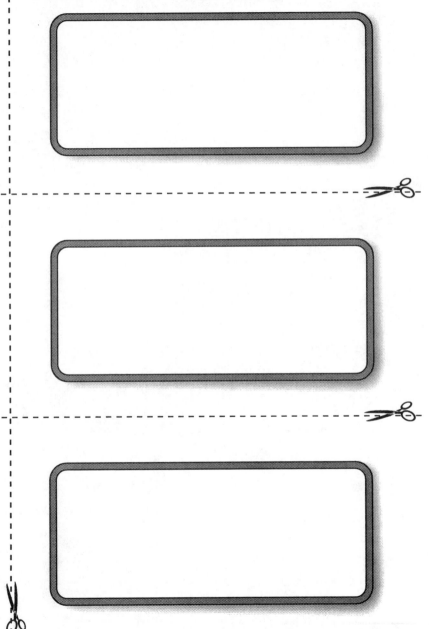

Correct Answers

Blank Cards for *Your Own Questions*

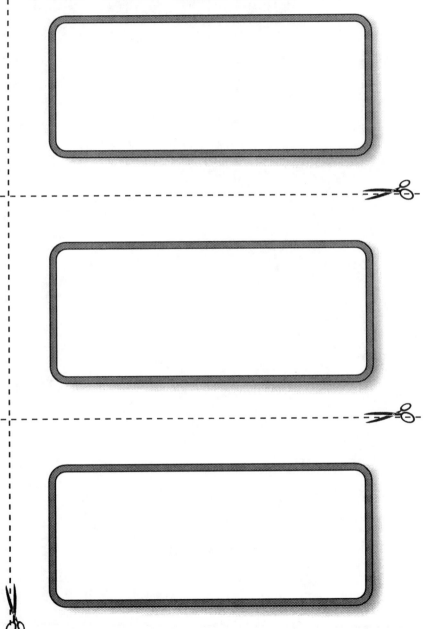

Correct Answers

Blank Cards for
Your Own Questions

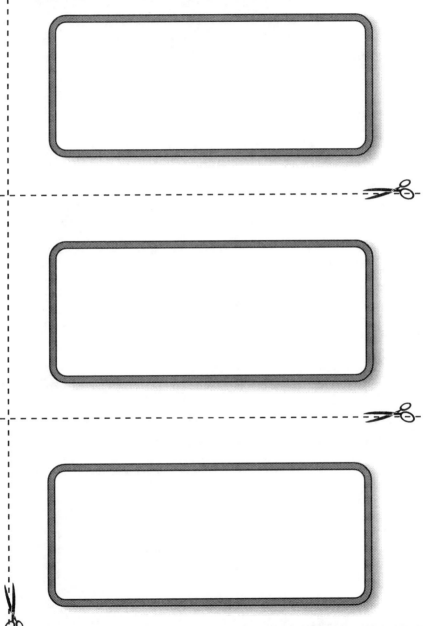

Correct Answers

Blank Cards for *Your Own Questions*

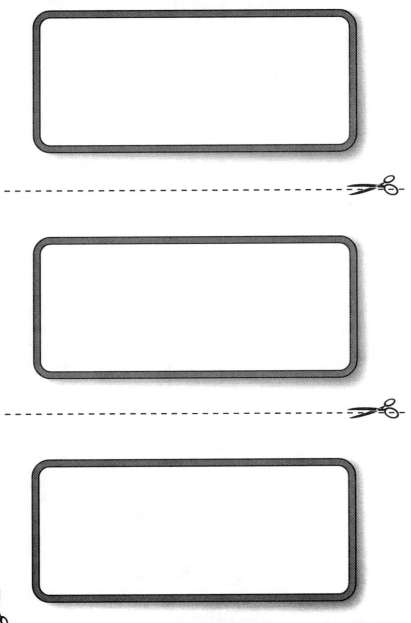

Correct Answers

Blank Cards for *Your Own Questions*

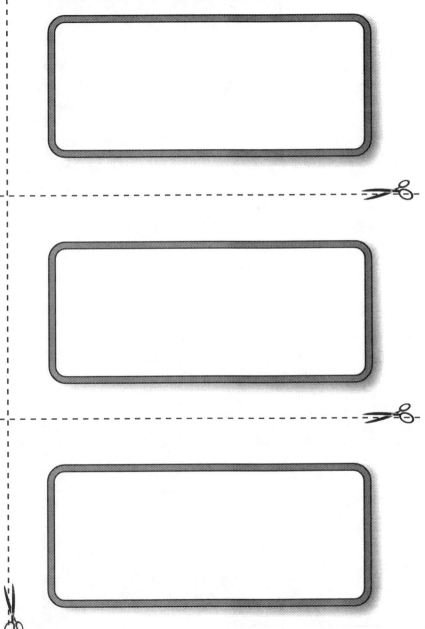

Correct Answers

Blank Cards for *Your Own Questions*

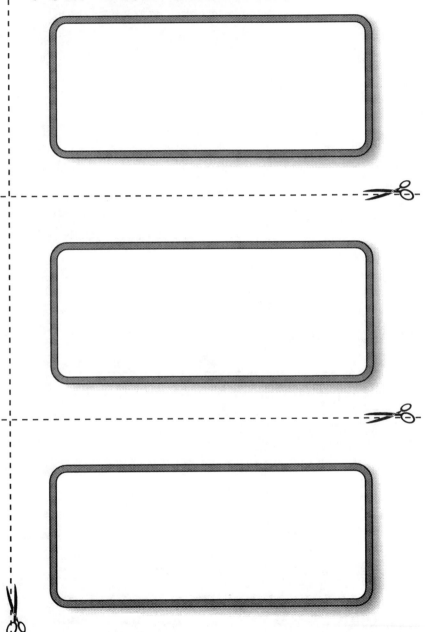

Correct Answers

Blank Cards for
Your Own Questions

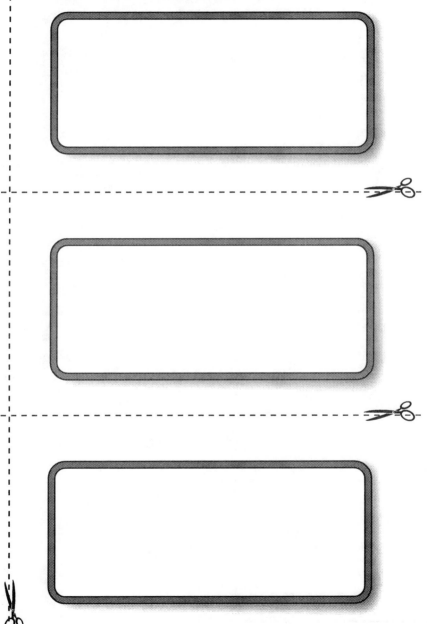

Correct Answers

Blank Cards for *Your Own Questions*

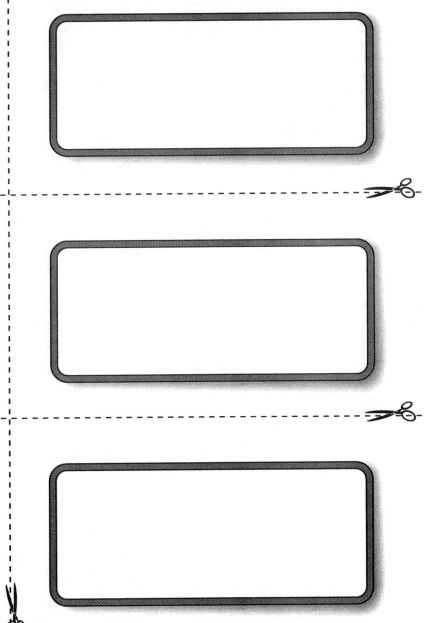

Correct Answers

Blank Cards for *Your Own Questions*

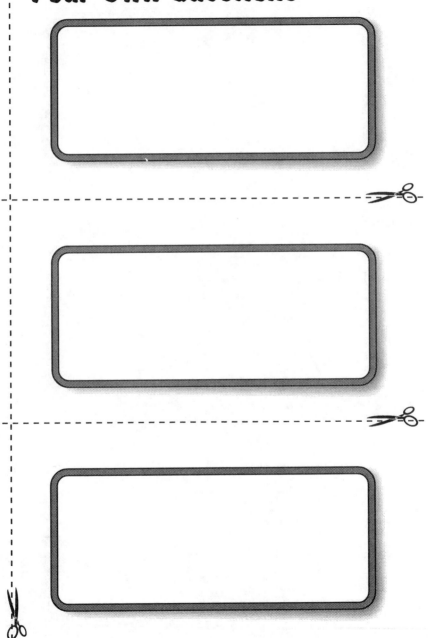

Correct Answers

Blank Cards for *Your Own Questions*

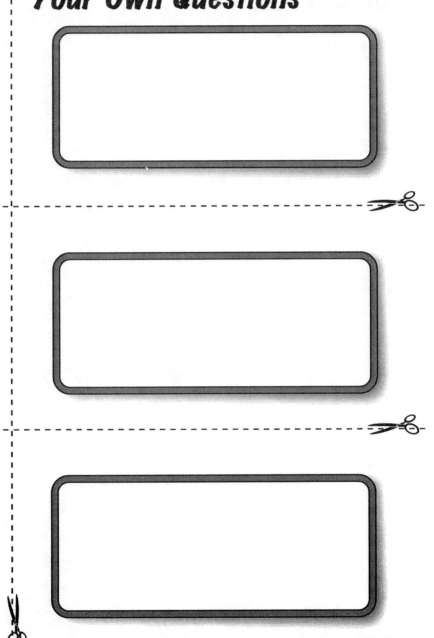

Correct Answers

Blank Cards for
Your Own Questions

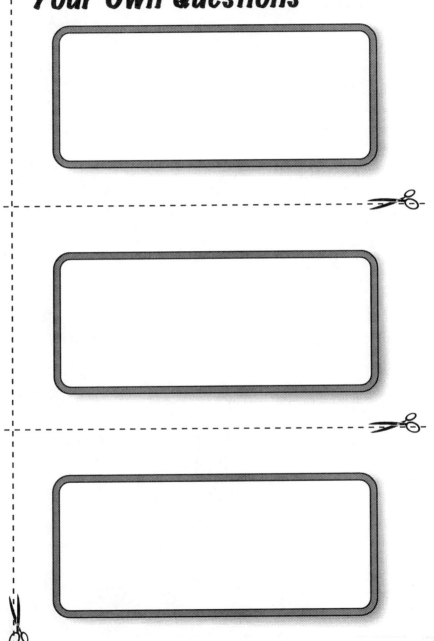

Correct Answers

INDEX